INTRODUCTION

Tzorchei Tzibbur: Community and Responsibility in the Jewish Tradition is a source and activity book designed to combine study and action. The Rabbis of the Talmud questioned the relative values of midrash (study) and ma'aseh (action), and determined that study is preferable to action only inasmuch as study leads to greater involvement in performing mitzvot. *Tzorchei Tzibbur* is based on this rabbinic premise and on the notion that the best way to teach people how to do something is *to do it*.

Each chapter is this study program conforms to three basic areas of procedure.

1. Initially, students become acquainted with traditional Jewish sensitivities toward specific groups of people with needs to be fulfilled; they compare their own feelings about these groups to traditional additudes; they determine areas of need that they might be able to satisfy and then plan projects to involve themselves in attempts to help those who are in need.

2. Next students implement the projects, developing relationships with community agencies and/or individuals who require their help.

3. Finally, students return to the texts of Jewish tradition and react to them in the light of the experience of giving of themselves.

The traditional sources are used in a number of ways: often they confront or encourage students' feelings; frequently they introduce new ideas and attitudes toward communal responsibility. On some occasions, the sources are presented with information about their historical origins and background; on others, they stand as timeless indicators of Jewish attitudes and values. The sources are seen as a means to two ends: as they are provocative and inspirational, they may spur action on the part of the students; as they represent problems that face our students today, they link together Jewish generations of the past and present.

Throughout *Tzorchei Tzibbur*, traditional sources are quoted in
an attempt to use the past to help to plan for the future. It
should be noted that not all of the texts found in the students'
material are included in the teaching strategies of this guide.
You may choose to work with texts you find especially appealing,
incorporate additional textual references, or encourage students
to consider the other material on their own. Generally, the
primary sources are provided for the values they embody, and so
this teacher's guide does not delve into the find points of
analyzing each textual reference, as important as that may be.

Students may wonder: What is Jewish about visiting the sick,
offering hospitality, or comforting mourners? *Tzorchei Tzibbur*
utilizes traditional texts to respond to this question:
tzedakah and gemilut ḥasadim are deeply rooted in the character
of the Jewish people. Furthermore, showing concern for the
needs of others--and for one's own needs--is a mitzvah, a
standard of behavior that guides Jews in their relationships
with each other and with the rest of the world. Although our
"copyright" on these sensitive behaviors has expired, nevertheless, we as Jews bring to community service some special
concerns.

We support the poor through a system of self-taxation. We
extend gemilut ḥasadim beyond the sphere of our friends and
acquaintances: we welcome strangers into our communities and
homes; we visit people we do not know when they are ill; we
ransom captives even if we have no previous experience with
them personally. Simply knowing that others are in need
forces the Jewish people to act on their behalf. Furthermore,
no other people has developed so comprehensive a body of legislation for dealing with the sensitivity of individual and
community toward those in need. Judaism legislates--*requires,
demands*--of Jews what others may choose to do. These qualifi-
cations of the Jewish involvement in serving our fellows do
not make us better or worse than other people. Most simply
put, THEY MAKE US JEWS.

As a result of participating in the study program presented
by *Tzorchei Tzibbur*, students should be able to

1. cite examples of how traditional Jewish texts relate to
       incidents in their own lives;

2. list examples of how the needs of individuals are con-
       sidered to be the needs of the Jewish community;

3. list the means by which Jews historically attempted to
       meet the needs of the poor, the captive, the sick,
       the mourner, the stranger, and the elderly, and
       compare them to the ways in which modern Jewish
       communities try to meet those needs;

4. list examples of how Jews have encouraged sensitivity
    both to the living and the dead;

5. participate as a group in community service projects
    related to the topics of each chapter;

6. write personal reactions to traditional texts after
    participating in community service projects.

In addition, it is hoped that

1. students will be inspired to emulate the historical
    models--both of personality and of process--that
    they study;

2. students will decide, either now or in the future, to
    become involved in a personal community service
    project from among the acts of tzedakah and gemilut
    ḥasadim they will have studied;

3. the relationship between the traditional texts in this
    study program and the interests of the students will
    be sufficiently meaningful for students to want to
    continue studying Jewish texts in the future; and

4. students will be impressed by the concerns of Jews of
    the past and present and will feel proud about
    being a link in the chain of Jewish tradition.

1.   Do not ask students to do things that you are unwilling to do yourself. This rule applies throughout the study program, including such issues as discussing your feelings and experiences openly and being willing to volunteer your time to visit the sick, comfort mourners, etc. Consider how *you* will be involved before you decide what you will require from students.

2.   The program of *Tzorchei Tzibbur* requires *study* and *action*. To be most effective, students and teachers should participate in the *action* as well as in the *study*. If such participation is impossible, you will have to utilize other approaches to the materials in the student source book inasmuch as the suggested strategies may not be appropriate.

3.   It is not only desirable but is absolutely necessary for participants to exchange feelings and experiences with each other, relating to the study topics of *Tzorchei Tzibbur*.

4.   In the same way that *Tzorchei Tzibbur* seeks to sensitize students to the needs of others outside of the educational setting, it also seeks to increase the sensitivity of class participants for each other. The teacher-student and student-student relationships in class should exemplify the principle of Ahavat HaBriot--love of one's fellows--expressed in the sources and derived from the community service activities. Teachers should try to model these sensitivities in their relationships with students. In an atmosphere of teacher respect for students' needs, students may begin to imitate the teacher's behaviors of acceptance and openess.

5.   Be truthful about your own responses to the issues. Remember that students need not adopt your viewpoint as their own--but that your feelings are important, too!

6.   Throughout this instructional guide, the term "teacher" or "advisor" is applied to anyone taking the role of educator or discussion leader. The terms "student" or "participant" are also used interchangeably, as are "class" and "group." However, every group using this material (whether in an informal educational setting, such as a USY chapter, or in a more formal school setting) will have to decide what methods are most appropriate for its own needs and schedule.

After students have participated in doing an activity related to the theme described in each chapter, they should be given class time to re-read the texts that originally appeared in the study program and to react to them in a personal way. This activity is based on the assumption that the relationship in Jewish tradition between midrash and ma'aseh works in two directions. That is, studying texts may motivate us to act upon their suggestions, but participating in the acts that the texts encourage may give us new insights into the meaning of the texts with which we began the learning process.

Therefore, as a summary of each study program, students will have the opportunity to read (some of) the texts they learned earlier in the program and to write comments on the texts, based on their own experience. Students should be encouraged to keep the sourcebook that contains their comments, and to review the texts and comments from time to time, to ascertain whether their attitudes have changed--and to ask themselves why. The texts are reproduced in the Appendix, where space has been provided for the students' written reactions to them.

In addition, the looseleaf format of *Tzorchei Tzibbur* should be used to full benefit, both in the Appendix and for various exercises and projects in each of the chapters.

As an introduction to subsequent chapters in this study program, *Tzorchei Tzibbur*, this lesson deals with the differentiation in Jewish tradition between צְדָקָה (tzedakah) and גְּמִילוּת חֲסָדִים (gemilut ḥasadim). As a result of studying this chapter, participants will be able to divide acts of community service into acts of tzedakah and gemilut ḥasadim. They will also be able to define tzedakah and gemilut ḥasadim.

Outline of Chapter:

1. Students list "what are the essential elements of a good life that you would not want to live without?"

2. Share with the class at least one of the elements. Would you want to provide the same elements for others?

3. Text study: Leviticus 19:18: וְאָהַבְתָּ לְרֵעֲךָ כָּמוֹךָ ("Love your neighbor as yourself").

4. Give concrete examples of how to fulfill Leviticus 19:18.

5. Text study: Sukkah 49b: acts of tzedakah and gemilut ḥasadim. Relate these concepts to Leviticus 19:18.

6. Differentiate traditional actions of the community for the individual according to tzedakah or gemilut ḥasadim.

7. Differentiate between tzedakah and gemilut ḥasadim for "essential elements" that are important to students that they could help others to acquire/achieve.

8. Summary: Define tzedakah and gemilut ḥasadim.

1. Ask students to turn to page 3 in the sourcebook and to do the exercise at the top of the page.

2. Ask each student to choose one of the "elements" which is most important and to explain to the rest of the class why it is important. Following the sharing, ask

KEY QUESTION: Do you believe other people think it is important to have these "elements," too, or do you think it is only your need to have them?

Following the responses, ask another

KEY QUESTION: Would you want other people to have the same "elements" or blessings as yours? Which other people?

3. Read the verse on page 3: "Love your neighbor as yourself." Ask students to explain what this means. What kind of love is involved? Who is the neighbor? What is it about yourself that you would want to be able to give to someone else? Read one (or both) of the contexts of "Love your neighbor as yourself" from the Torah. How does the context help you to define the love, the neighbor, and the aspects of yourself?

Note the restatement of the idea by Hillel, probably 1000 years later. How does this formulation change the meaning--or does it?

4. Explain to students how to fill out the chart at the bottom of page 3 and apply it to the verse "Love your neighbor as your-self" as follows: if the element is "a good job," how could we show love to another person who also wants "a good job"? Who might the other person be? Does he have to be a neighbor? Would there have to be a special relationship between us? How would our treatment of someone else who also wants a "good job" be like the treatment you would like to receive, or would give to yourself? The chart might look something like this:

Element	Love	Another person (your neighbor)	Like yourself
A good job	Help to get a job. Make a job working with or for me a "good" one--a pleasant experience.	Someone I might not know at the begin- ning but I surely would know if I worked with him.	Be fair to him. Be pleasant and not mean. Be able to ad- vance in his work.

Ask students to choose two or three of the essential elements they have listed and to apply them to the notion that someone else might want something they have.

SUMMARIZE this section: Ask students to consider how it feels to recognize that something they value a great deal might also be valued by other people.

5. Tell students that the Jewish people has had a number of ways of showing love for one another and for other people. Two very important ways of showing this love have been through tzedakah and gemilut ḥasadim. If they do not know what these words mean, we will define them in a little while. For the time being, we will use the Hebrew terms and try to do some detective work to discover what they might mean in English.

Read the text from Sukkah 49b. The text is written in three parallel sets of ideas, each of which includes a definition of what tzedakah includes and what gemilut ḥasadim includes. Read each set. Stop. Ask students to think of examples of each stipulation. Then go on to repeat for each set.

Example: What might be a case in which a person needs help, but receiving a gift of money would be all the help he needs? What case might describe needing more than money?

List the cases that students suggest as examples of each clause on the board under the two headings.

Below is a sketch of what the list on the board might look like:

Gemilut Ḥasadim	Tzedakah
--giving money	--giving money (or food or clothes)
--giving hospitality to friends whose house was destroyed by fire	--giving money (or food or clothes) to the poor
--giving money or food or clothes to the poor	--giving money (or food or clothes) to the poor who are living
--reading to a wealthy blind person	
--giving money or food or clothes to the poor who are living	(Note: the category of tzedakah may be expanded to include physical properties, such as food or clothing.)
--burying someone who has died	

Ask students to describe what has happened to the category of tzedakah. (Essentially, it was been swallowed up by gemilut ḥasadim.) Read the text on page 4 from the Jerusalem Talmud (the Yerushalmi). Ask students a KEY QUESTION: How does this text help to differentiate between tzedakah and gemilut ḥasadim?

Those acts of גמ"ח (an abbreviation for gemilut ḥasadim) which require one's material goods could be defined as tzedakah. Those which require personal service make up the rest of the category of גמ"ח. How do all of the acts that we have discussed relate to the notion of "Love your neighbor as yourself"? (You may want to refer students to the text at the top of page 4 from Pirkay Avot that states that whatever we have, material goods or personal abilities, belongs to God.)

Why would individual Jews want to do acts of either tzedakah or gemilut ḥasadim?

Why would a community of Jews want to do these acts?

Today, many individual Jews do acts of tzedakah and gemilut ḥasadim.

Jewish communities are also organized to do these acts: Federations, synagogues, and other Jewish organizations work to fulfill the needs of Jews who need money or personal service.

Assign students to research what the Jewish organizations (Federation, B'nai Brith, etc.) do to help the needy in their communities.

6. Ask students to skim the text on page 5. If they have questions about what they have read, discuss their problems and allow the group an opportunity to respond to the questions before you answer (your answer may then be unnecessary!).

Ask participants to examine carefully the chart on page 6,
and to fill it out in pairs (students sitting closest to each
other).

Discuss the responses to the chart when the students have
finished. Be aware that the traditional definitions of tzedakah
and gemilut ḥasadim are ambiguous (since some sources provide
partially conflicting definitions). Allow students some leeway
in their responses, as long as they can support their
categorizations.

7. Ask students to do the work on page 7 individually.

   A. Point out that both gemilut ḥasadim and tzedakah are מִצְוֹת (mitzvot).

   B. Be sure students know what a מִצְוָה is. Definitions of the concept of mitzvah vary and generally depend on one's orientation to halachah (Jewish law).

      Simply speaking, two possible approaches are embodied in these definitions:

         1. a commandment

         2. standard for the behavior of the Jewish people.

      (Other nuances and interpretations are possible.)

      For a more detailed treatment of the issues involved, refer to Elliot N. Dorff, Conservative Judaism: Our Ancestors to Our Descendants (New York: United Synagogue Youth, 1977), especially Chapter III.

   C. Briefly discuss with the class your own and/or other definitions of the concept of mitzvah.

   D. Summarize the introductory lesson by asking students to read their definitions of tzedakah and gemilut hasadim. You may then wish to consider if either of the two might be considered "more important" than the other.

This chapter is divided into three units that deal with the subject of bringing guests into one's home.

It is assumed that all students have had some experience being a host and being a guest, and that some of these experiences have been positive, while others have not. The major objective of this chapter is to enable students to list the behaviors required of a host in order to ensure that his guest is comfortable, and to use the list as a guide in planning future activities that include hospitality, either in its traditional sense of hosting a guest at home, or in a broader sense, of welcoming guests to the classroom, youth group, or social group of which students are members. In addition, students will be able to

1) define different kinds of hospitality that are found in biblical and rabbinic traditions;

2) analyze the interaction of hosts and guests in the clasroom framework.

A major assumption of this chapter is that a classroom or discussion group can be similar to a home, and that a teacher is the initial classroom host. Ideally, the students will begin to consider the classroom to be a property that both the teacher and they share. When that is the case, a number of things can be expected to happen. Most obviously, the students and the teacher will all have to function as hosts when dealing with visitors or guests in the classroom--and all will have to make decisions about how to treat guests and whom to invite or welcome. Perhaps less clearly, students will begin to accept responsibility for what happens in the classroom. Whether or not this occurs depends to a great extent upon the personality of the teacher and his willingness to allow students to play a role in decision-making. This openness may build an atmosphere that not only encourages sharing of responsibility for hospitality in the class but also calls for students to share responsibility for the success of other group projects and ideas.

This chapter is written for teenagers who have spent at least eight years in a variety of classroom settings. Many of them will know from the outset in what kinds of settings they are likely to learn and in which settings their learning processes are inhibited. Others may not have such sophisticated ideas about education and will need to experience models of different kinds of learning environments in order to see clearly what their own needs are. We do not say that students alone should dictate class atmosphere, methods, and subject matter; but we are saying that if the classroom is supposed to be the "turf" of both the leader and the participants, then both should have a hand in deciding what kind of activities ought to be encouraged or permitted on this "turf."

<u>Unit 1:</u> Students should be able to list a number of ways and circumstances under which Jews welcomed guests or strangers into their homes.

<u>Outline of Unit:</u>

1. Introductory activity.

2. Anecdote and personal judgment about how to treat a stranger in the synagogue.

3. Text study: Why and how have Jews practiced Hachnasat Orḥim.

4. Historical perspective: How was the ancient world different from our world in terms of the needs of strangers for hospitality?

5. Laws of Hachnasat Orḥim.

INTRODUCTORY ACTIVITY

Set the stage for the discussion of how to offer hospitality by creating in the classroom an atmosphere of warm hospitality to students (during the first half of the first class session) and an atmosphere of apathy and disinterest in students (during the second half of the session). The purpose of the activity is to give students an immediate first-hand experience of the way differing attitudes toward guests feel--when they are the guests.

I. Suggestions for creating the atmosphere of warm hospitality.

    A. *Form:* Play soft, relaxing music in the room. Welcome each student at the door, greeting him personally, commenting on how well he looks or on good work he has done, etc. Serve refreshments--cookies and juice will suffice. Arrange seating informally, perhaps even with pillows on the floor. Allow this atmosphere to prevail for about half the class session. Then give students a five minute break. Say goodbye to each student personally as he leaves the room. Express your pleasure that he was able to attend the session, and tell him how much it means to you to have him as a student. (After the break, when students return, you will attempt to set a negative atmosphere.)

    B. *Content:* During the time of warm hospitality toward students, begin the work of the unit on Hachnasat Orḥim (see page T- 11). The intellectual atmosphere of the class should be (as always) accepting of divergent opinions and new ideas. Such acceptance will at to the atmosphere of cordial hospitality you are trying to create.

II. Suggestions for setting the unpleasant atmosphere.

    A. *Form:* Set up seats in a random, disorganized style. Come into the class late, show anger for students who wander in after you do. Don't call students by their names. "Hey you" wil suffice. Don't allow socializing of any kind. Do not allow students to get out of their seats for any reason. Act generally unhappy about the prospect of spending the class time with these students.

    B. *Content:* Inasmuch as students may associate their bad feelings about the way your are treating them with the content of the lesson, choose some subject matter that will not suffer greatly if students consider it boring and associate bad feelings with it. Some possibilities might include

                memorizing the names of the kings of Israel, in order;
                reading an encyclopedia-type article.

During this time enforce strict and inflexible discipline; try to be as unpleasant as you can!

III. Debriefing the two atmospheres of hospitality created in class.

After the first 10 of 15 minutes of the unpleasant atmosphere, stop the content activity and ask students to discuss the way you treated them during the first part of the session and the way you treated them during the second part of the session.

List the behaviors they recall in two columns on the blackboard. Leave space between the two columns for two other lists: How did students feel in response to your behaviors that generated the "warm" atmosphere, and how did they feel in response to your behaviors that generated the "unpleasant" atmosphere? Note your own feelings as a result of their behavior.

Discuss how these two kinds of atmosphere are related to hospitality. Encourage students to relate incidents from their lives that demonstrate the need for guests to reciprocate with appreciation. Ask students to discuss a synectic exercise: How is a classroom like a home?

> *NOTE:* Synectic exercises consist of comparing two generally dissimilar items to learn more about each. Example: How is halachah like a rubber band?

UNIT 1

1. **Anecdote and personal judgment about how to treat a stranger in the synagogue.**

   Ask students to read the anecdote on page 11. They should answer the questions about it, or act out the situation, role-playing the incident, creating an ending. Different groups may create different endings. Discuss their responses. Ask students to hypothesize about reasons the stranger might be in the synagogue. Some possibilities that should be discussed are that

   a. he is new in town and came to the synagogue because he thinks it is a good place to meet people.

   b. he was on his way home when his car broke down. Since he is Shomer Shabbat, he came to the synagogue hoping that someone would invite him home for Shabbat.

   c. he is a traveler who is in town for only a short stay. He likes to learn about Jewish communities that he visits and hopes someone will offer him hospitality.

   Ask students if they know of any incidents that have actually occured that are like the one described or any of those about which they have hypothesized. Have they ever been in a strange place and wished that someone would befriend them?

2. **Text study: Why and how have Jews practiced Hachnasat Orḥim?**

   Ask students to read the text from Genesis 18 (about Abraham) on page 11. Has Abraham done anything special in this incident? Would every desert dweller run to welcome a complete stranger? Three strangers? Why or why not?

   What does Abraham do for his guests? How do you think his hospitality impressed them? How would it rank against our contemporary ideas about how to treat strangers? Do you think his hospitality was generous in its own historical milieu?

   Rabbinic tradition explains that one of the the three messengers visited Abraham as an act of Bikkur Ḥolim (visiting the sick). The Rabbis assume this visit to take place while Abraham is recuperating from his circumcision (Chapter 17). Although we are studying the Genesis 18 section to understand Hachnasat Orḥim, various values overlap, and are integrated (as mentioned in the *Introduction* to the students' sourcebook).

Jews have often admired the model of Abraham as a hospitable person. Why do you think Jews have been interested in being hospitable? Since the Jewish people has frequently been treated inhospitably by foreign governments and by their neighbors, wouldn't it make sense for us to show concern only for ourselves and not for others?

> (Ask students if it is true that Jews are often strangers and have been treated inhospitably.)

Ask students to read the text from Leviticus on page 11 . How did the Bible respond to the fact that the Israelites had been strangers in a foreign land? How were they supposed to treat other strangers now that they occupied their own land?

> To what period of Jewish history was Leviticus referring?

> Is this principle of treating others as we would like to be treated still valid today? What kind of world would we be helping to build if we say "no"? What kind of world would we be helping to build if we say "yes"?

Divide the class into four groups. Assign each group to read one of the first four texts on page 12. Ask each group to discuss

How does this text relate to the idea of Leviticus 19:33-34 (on page 11)?

Write this question on the blackboard so the groups may refer to it in order to stay on target in their discussions.

Allow about ten minutes for the discussion. Reconvene the class as a whole and ask representatives of each group to report by

1. summarizing the text on page 12 that the group studied, and

2. showing any relationships they found between their text and Leviticus 19:33-34, or noting why they could not find any relationship between the texts.

After each presentation, allow the other students to question group members and to discuss their own ideas about the text.

Ask students to read the short statement from the Jerusalem Talmud (Demai 4:3). Ask if they agree or disagree with the principle being taught. Toward whom does this text show sensitivity? What does it tell us about the limits of hospitality?

Ask students to read the Encyclopedia Judaica text on page 13 and to continue by reading the questions at the top of page 14.

3. Ask students to answer the questions on the top of page 14.
    Discuss the students' responses to the questions.

    The main point is that modernity has brought with it hotels,
    motels, hostels, dormitories, etc., that lodge travelers and
    students who are away from home. In general, though, these
    provisions fit the needs only of those who can afford them.
    Occasionally, even people who can afford to pay for lodging
    away from home have additional needs--for Shabbat and holiday
    celebration in the proper manner, for the atmosphere of family
    and friends--that are not satisfied by staying in hotels, etc.

    Read the Genesis 19:1-9 excerpt about Lot and the guests.

    What does this text tell us about the kind of reception a
    traveler in the ancient world could expect to receive when
    he arrived in a new city?

    Evaluate Abraham's and Lots' hospitality against the background
    of the intentions of the men of Sodom.

    Can you understand why Abraham and Lot are considered to be
    models of hospitable people?

Read through the time line on page 15.

Ask students the following questions:

a. How does even this brief survey of Jewish history indicate the need for hospitality to strangers and guests?

b. Why do you think Hachnasat Orḥim is part of gemilut ḥasadim?

c. If you had lived in any of these time periods, how would (do) you think you would have felt about sheltering strangers and offering hospitality to guests?

4. **Guidelines for Hachnasat Orḥim.**

Assign pairs of students to work together to read and discuss
the laws for Hachnasat Orḥim both from the point of view of
the host and of the guest (pages 16-17). One member of the
pair reads a rule for the host, tells what he thinks it means
or what kinds of situations it refers to, and the other reacts
to it, discussing his partner's perceptions of the text and
adding anything he can to understand it better. Then the
other reads a guideline for the guest and follows the same
procedure until the pair has completed discussing all of
the texts.

Encourage students to take notes in their books and list
questions they may have about the texts. Review the texts
and deal with questions at the beginning of the next
class session.

<u>Unit 2</u>: a. Students should be able to list traditional guidelines
           for inviting, entertaining, and escorting guests.

        b. Students should be able to compare and contrast
           traditional guidelines with their own perceptions of
           proper behavior of a host.

        c. Students will be able to list traditional guidelines
           for how guests should behave. They will compare these
           guidelines with their own perceptions of proper behavior
           of a guest and suggest possible reasons for the
           differences.

<u>Outline of Lesson:</u>

    1. Review guidelines from the previous session.

    2. Values continua: evaluating your own position.

    3. Consideration of modern realities.

    4. Write rules for inviting, entertaining, and
       escorting guests. Write explanatory comments.

    5. Compare and contrast: small group rules with
       guidelines from Jewish tradition.

    6. Plan to invite a guest to class. Decide upon
       format for the visit, etc.

UNIT 2

1. <u>Review guidelines from previous session.</u>

   Ask students to reread the texts on pages 16-17 one at a time, and allow them to raise their questions and to react to the texts.

   Read and discuss the anecdotes about Yannai and Bar Kamtza on pages 18-19. Use the questions following both stories and those below to guide the discussion. At the conclusion, ask students what additional rules they think should be added to the list as a result of the incidents involving Yannai and Bar Kamtza. Ask students to add those rules on page 17.

   <u>About the Leviticus Rabbah text</u>:

   What kind of person did Yannai want to invite to his home?
       (A great man; a scholar.)

   How was Yannai accustomed to treating his guests?
       (He fed them and quizzed their Jewish knowledge.)

   Is Yannai's request, "Wash your hands and say Birkat HaMazon" part of the "quiz"?
       (Probably. He wanted to know if his guest knew how to behave properly at a meal and if he knew how to recite Birkat HaMazon.)

   How did the guest do on Yannai's "quiz"?
       (He failed completely.)

   Why do you think Yannai asked the guest to repeat the words, "A dog has eaten from Yannai's bread"?
       (Yannai was angry that his guest not only was not a scholar but seemed to be completely ignorant of Jewish observance. Yannai must have considered the guest unworthy of his hospitality, since asking the guest to say that he was a dog was obviously an insult. Apparently, Yannai wanted his guest to know that he (the guest) did not live up to his (Yannai's) expectations.)

   How did the guest respond to the insult?
       (The guest explained to Yannai that both of them have an equal share in the inheritance of the Jewish people. Yannai's learning did not entitle him to demean others simply because they did not possess his knowledge. The Torah was given to all the people of Israel--not only the people of Yannai!)

   What did the guest do that impressed Yannai?
       (He explained his selfless concern for other people's sensitivities and for maintaining peace between people wherever he went.)

What lessons did Yannai learn as a result of his encounter with his guest?

Among other lessons are these:

1) Not to judge people by external appearances;

2) to offer hospitality without "strings attached";

3) people should treat each other with derech eretz (respect, manners, sensitivity);

4) to behave with derech eretz toward his guests.

2. Values continua: where do you stand? Evaluating your own
    position on the issues.

    Ask students to work individually marking their positions
    on the series of values continua. (Below the mark have
    each student write a brief description of his or her
    position.)

    Divide the class into groups of three or four and ask
    students to share their positions with the others in
    their group.

    After about ten minutes, tell students to take a moment
    to adjust any opinions on the continua that they may have
    changed during the small group discussions.

    OR

    Draw lines on the floor (use masking tape) for each
    continuum. Let the participants stand at the appropriate
    place on each continuum to mark their positions.

3. Consideration of Modern Realities

Since there is a network of hotels, motels, and restaurants all over the world, why would we need to offer any kind of hospitality to strangers?

Why would strangers be interested in our hospitality?

Is the Jewish *community* still involved in Hachnasat Orḥim (meeting the needs of new immigrants--including groups such as Soviet Jews--people who are newcomers having recently moved into town, etc.)?

As far as entertaining guests who are our friends, can we not assume that we would treat our guests pleasantly and that they would respond pleasantly to our hospitality?

Are rules for the guest-host relationship necessary?
Why or why not?

> (Have you ever felt uncomfortable because your host or guest didn't seem to understand your assumptions about what was supposed to happen during a visit?)

4. Write rules for inviting, entertaining, and escorting guests.

Ask students to return to their small groups and to turn to page 22. Ask them to work together to formulate a set of guidelines for each of the three parts of the hospitality process outlined there. Each group member should copy the group's guidelines into his own book. Ask participants to write explanations or commentaries for the rules they decide upon, to insure that they-- and others who might read them--will be able to remember exactly what they had in mind.

Each group should list its rules on a piece of oak tag or newsprint that will be used in "Compare and Contrast" below.

5. Compare and Contrast: student rules with traditional guidelines.

Reconvene the group as a whole. Post the lists of rules produced by the small groups (on newsprint or oak tag) in the front of the room. Which of the traditional ideas did not occur at all in the students' lists of guidelines? Ask students to discuss why they did not include these ideas. If any of the rules generated by different groups conflict, try to arrive at a consensus of one rule that the class in general will accept.

Which of the rules written by the class correspond directly to traditional texts they have studied? Which traditional texts? Note this information on the board next to each rule.

Which of the rules are related to traditional ideas but do not directly parallel a traditional text? Note the text with the same idea on the board.

Which of the rules are entirely unrelated to the ideas of the traditional texts? Why do students think these ideas were not expressed in the texts they studied? What modern conditions might require these guidelines? Circle these rules on the board.

Refer to page 14 and students' lists of "The need for Hachnasat Orḥim." To which needs have students' lists of rules responded? Should additional rules be considered because of existence of needs students may have overlooked?

6. Plan to invite a guest to class.

    Tell students that they have compiled a meaningful list of
    guidelines and that you think they ought to try them out
    to see if they will work--if they will produce a   success-
    ful and pleasant visit. Ask them to utilize the guidelines
    generated by the class to help invite, entertain, and say
    goodbye to a guest. Plan to invite the guest for the next
    class session.*

    * (The guest should be invited to spend only part of the
       session with the group so that students will have time
       to evaluate the visit and to plan subsequent activities
       of hospitality.)

    Discuss the best way to work on this plan with the parti-
    cipants. The whole class can work together on all decision-
    making and planning or committees can be appointed to deal
    with different aspects of the visit (i.e., inviting, plan-
    ning what will happen during the visit, refreshments, saying
    goodbye). Invite only one or two guests for this session.
    Spend the rest of the session planning for the visit.

    Note that any expenses incurred by the class for the visit
    should be shared by all class members (and leader).

Unit 3:   a.   Students should be able to evaluate the success
              of a visit based on their own rules and traditional
              Jewish guidelines.

         b.   Students should be able to utilize their own and
              traditional guidelines to plan a Kinnus, to invite
              peers to spend a weekend in their homes and
              synagogues.

Outline of Unit

1.   Entertain a guest.

2.   Discuss how class members felt about the visit.
     How did it line up with traditional values?
     With small group values?

3.   Plan a group activity for Hachnasat Orḥim.

1. Entertain the guest.
   Carry out the visit as it has been planned by the students.

2. Discussion: How did the visit measure up to traditional Jewish notions of a successful visit? to the guidelines drawn up by the group?

   When the guest leaves, ask students to fill out the form on page 23, *Analyzing a Visit*. Students should do this work individually. Allow about 10-15 minutes for this work.

   Review each section of analysis and ask students to share their perceptions and analyses with the whole group.

   What aspects of the visit were as good as they could be? Why do you think they turned out to be so pleasant?

   In what other situations do students--as individuals or as members of a group--have to be hosts?

3. Plan a Group Activity for Hashnasat Orhim.

   Ask students if they think the guidelines they have drawn up would work in a home situation as well as in a class situation. Discuss any modifications that would have to be made.

   Discuss how the class could have the opportunity to try out their hospitality guidelines in their own homes or elsewhere. If no one else mentions it, suggest inviting students from a neighboring town or USY chapter to spend Shabbat or the entire weekend in your community as guests of the participants. Other similar activities or variations can be considered.

   Repeat the procedure for planning to invite a guest to class, only this time the planning must be done on a grander scale, to include all-day scheduling, meals, how to handle expenses, parental permission, etc.

   Suggest a planning framework to students:
   1. What are the needs of guests?
   2. Analyze the needs of guests
      a. Which can be satisfied.
      b. Which cannot be satisfied.
   3. Which of the needs that can be satisfied should be the focus of the visit?
   4. How can the program reflect this focus?

   At the conclusion of the kinnus, ask both your group and the visiting group to evaluate the event. Ask your students to discuss the notion of Hachnasat Orhim with their guests. Ask both groups to relate the events of the kinnus to the guidelines of the tradition and of the class.

VISITING THE SICK--BIKKUR ḤOLIM--בִּקּוּר חוֹלִים

Bikkur Ḥolim is a mitzvah that people of all ages and social standings can practice. The objective of this unit of study is to enable students to form a חֶבְרַת בִּקּוּר חוֹלִים (Ḥevrat Bikkur Ḥolim--Society for Visiting the Sick) and practice this important mitzvah on a regular basis. In forming the Ḥevrah for the group, students will write a constitution that includes guidelines how to go about visiting the sick. Students will be encouraged to take into account both rabbinic attitudes for Bikkur Ḥolim and their own feelings and beliefs about what is proper treatment for the sick. In the process of achieving this objective, students will be able to

1. identify different kinds of illnesses and the care they require;

2. compare and contrast their own ideas about visiting the sick with the ideas of rabbinic tradition; and

3. describe their feelings when they have to depend on someone else in order to do commonplace activities (as the sick must often do as a result of their illnesses).

This study program is divided into three units:

Unit 1
1. Empathy-inducing experience.
2. Discussion of dependence.
3. Categorizing illnesses.
4. Text study.

Unit 2
1. Empathy-inducing experience.
2. Text study.

Unit 3
1. Discussion: the involvement of the Jewish community in sick care.
2. Formation of a Bikkur Ḥolim Society and writing its constitution.

NOTE: *There may be some students who are seriously ill or who have close relatives who are seriously ill.* One way to find out if there are such problems among your students is to consult the rabbi prior to beginning this unit. He may have suggestions for how to treat the student(s) and the situation(s) in the context of studying Bikkur Ḥolim. Try to utilize the rabbi as a resource for other aspects of the *Tzorchei Tzibbur* program as well. Prior to beginning this unit, speak to these individuals privately. Ask them if and how they want to participate in the

unit. If they prefer not to be present in the class while
Bikkur Ḥolim is discussed, make the necessary arrangements that
will show sensitivity to their needs. Such students could
prove to be a valuable resource--IF THEY WANT TO BE. If they
do not want to be involved, pressuring them to do so could cause
serious emotional damage.

Some options for that to do if these students to not want to be
involved in class sessions:

1. Prepare individualized materials based on the
    sources provided in this chapter. Allow the
    students to work alone--at home or in the library.

2. Ask them to write about their own experiences
    that are related to Bikkur Ḥolim.

3. Suggest reading materials that may be helpful
    to these students as they face their problems.
    Fiction or non-fiction may be considered,
    depending on the specific problems, needs, and
    sensitivities of the individuals.

4. Let these students guide you. Don't pressure
    them; offer options. Indicate a sincere willing-
    ness to listen, to spend time with them, to be
    satisfied with the choices that make them
    feel comfortable.

1. **Empathy-inducing experience.**

   Randomly select half the students to receive "handicaps" that they will bear during the first class session. During the second class session,* the other half of the class will receive "handicaps." During the "discussion of dependence" (third class session), students will have the opportunity to discuss how they felt both as the "handicapped" and as the helpers of the "handicapped." "Handicaps" should be relatively simple constraints on some aspect of the students' independence. These might include blindfolds, ear plugs, or immobilizing the dominant hand. Students who are "handicapped" will have difficulty participating in group activities. Those who are not "handicapped" should be free do help the others if they wish to do so.

   * *Note: Should your schedule necessitate, you may choose to divide one class period rather than extending this activity over several sessions.*

2. **Discussion of Dependence.**

   a. Ask students to share their feelings about what aspects of being handicapped they disliked and what aspects they thought were not so bad. Ask them to discuss how they felt when they were not handicapped but had the opportunity to help others who were. What were the negative aspects of that experience, and what were some of the good feelings they had?

   b. Ask students what they consider to be the best way to live--being independent of or dependent on others? Introduce the notion of *INTERDEPENDENCE*--sharing responsibilities and needs with others who share with you. Read the selection on page 29 to clarify this basic attitude. Do any students consider interdependence to be the best foundation on which to build human relationships? What are the advantages and disadvantages of interdependence?

   c. How does knowing that the Jewish community cherishes the value of helping those in need make you feel--as a potential recipient of the help? --as a donor, representing the community? Does the Jewish value of helping those in need represent a position on the dependence-interdependence issue? Use ideas you have studied from Jewish tradition to prove what you believe about the values of the Jewish community.

   d. If you are healthy and financially well-to-do, is it possible to live without depending on anyone else for anything? Is it desirable? What do we add to our lives when we engage in acts of community reponsibility like Bikkur Ḥolim? How does Bikkur Ḥolim relate to "Love your neighbor as yourself"?

   e. *Summary:* You have engaged in an exercise that has made clear some of the areas in life in which we may need the cooperation of others. You have seen, if only by means of simulated handicaps, that from time to time everyone needs the help of someone else. For that reason and for others, Judaism beckons us to be that someone else for another person who needs US--each and every one of us.

3. Categorizing Illnesses

a.   Ask students to list illnesses they know something about or have heard about. List these on the board.

b.   Ask students to note, next to each illness, the kind of professional care a patient might need if he had this illness. Then discuss what other needs a patient might have that might not benefit from professional care. If students do not raise the issue of "support from friends and community" or "help to do basic life activities that the patient was able to do prior to the illness," then ask: "Would a patient need to feel that someone was concerned about his welfare?" How might he get that feeling?" or "Would the patient have any needs precipitated by the illness that he would not have had prior to the illness?" Allow students to work out how different illnesses cause differing needs to those who are afflicted. For example, does a recently blinded person usually need the same kind of support that a cancer patient requires? Pick a few examples of this type and encourage students to discuss what kind of help or care is required.

c.   Have students divide the illnesses into any categories that seem to be natural differentiators (i.e., the simplest categories might be "physical illness," "mental illness," "permanent handicaps"; other differentiations could include "acute illnesses," "chronic illnesses," "illnesses from which recovery is expected," "illnesses that are expected to be fatal," "illnesses that do not require hospitalization," etc.). Depending upon the categories the students define, ask them to divide the illnesses they have listed into the appropriate categories. Ask if they have thought of additional illnesses that they would like to add. Does the category of the illness indicate anything about the care required?

d.   Encourage students to discuss the way they generally feel when they are ill, and what kinds of things make them feel better or help them recover more quickly.

e.   Have participants record the list on the board onto page 30 in the sourcebook.

f.   Tell students that we are going to study some rabbinic texts that discuss the way Jews have traditionally visited the sick and the reasons for doing so. Ask them to keep in mind the discussion of different illnesses that require different care so that they can try out their ideas against the thoughts of the Rabbis.

See if students woild like to invite a rabbi (or hospital chaplain) to meet with them to discuss how he goes about visiting the sick, and what he does, says, etc. If the group would like to include this element of personal input in their discussions, appoint a committee to decide upon whom to invite and how to extend the invitation (using guidelines from the unit on Hachnasat Orḥim). Time should be set aside for the visit of the rabbi during the next class session. And/Or see if students would like to interview someone who has gone through a lengthy rehabilitation process at a hospital, to share experiences and feelings with the group.

4a. <u>Text study: Why visit the sick?</u>

i. Read the first line of the text on page 31 (Nedarim 39b) that begins "Rabbi Aḥa son of Ḥanina." Ask students to react to the idea that each person who visits an invalid takes away 1/60 of his illness. Is it true? What could the Rabbis have had in mind? If someone believed this idea, then what would he do every time someone got sick? (Bring in 60 visitors.) Would bringing in 60 visitors help to cure all of the types of illness we defined previously? What harm might it do to bring 60 visitors to see some people who are sick?

ii. Read the remainder of the text. The Rabbis indicated that every visitor decreases the <u>remaining part</u> of the illness by 1/60, thereby indicating that regardless of how many people visit an invalid, he will still be sick. (This works on the same principle as the support daughters receive from their father's estate. According to Jewish tradition, when a man dies, his son inherits his property. The son, however, must contribute a tenth of his inheritance to the support of each of his sisters as they marry. If a man had ten sisters, would he be left with no inheritance? The Rabbis say: No. The principle involves taking a tenth of the <u>remainder</u>, not an absolute tenth of the estate.)

Do you think the Rabbis considered a person's illness actually to decrease because many people came to visit him? What do you think they were trying to teach in this text?
> (Possible responses: if an invalid feels that people care about his welfare, it makes him feel better; many visitors may take a person's mind off his pain; many visitors make the time pass more quickly and the invalid may not notice how long he has been sick; they may provide a link to the outside healthy world.)

iii. Read the selection that begins "Rav Ḥelbo fell ill." What was it that Rabbi Akiba did for his disciple? How could this action have caused the man to recover? Do you agree with Akiba's conclusion: "He who does not visit the sick is like a shedder of blood"?

iv. Read the selection that begins "When Rav Dimi came." How does Rav Dimi explain Akiba's conclusion?

v. *SUMMARIZE*: According to the Rabbis, why should we visit the sick?

4b. **Text Study: When and how long to visit?**

i. Read the selection on page 32 beginning "Rav Shisha son of Rav Idi." What are the two reasons given for not visiting the sick during the first and last three hours of the day? Why shouldn't a visitor see the invalid when he is feeling best or worst?

> (Possible responses: if he sees him during the first three hours, he might think that the invalid is nearly well and not in need of visitors. If he visits during the last three hours, he might think the patient is about to die. In either case, the temporary change in the invalid's condition might cause the visitor to treat him in ways that are inappropriate to his condition.)

Isn't this common sense? Why do you think the Rabbis felt the need to say it explicitly?

ii. Read the selection by Rabbi Eliezer (b. Isaac of Worms). What are the conditions that might make him counsel visitors in this way? Why are "the patient's eyes on those who come in"? Relate this statement to the comfort given by Rabbi Akiba (on page 31). Was it the fact that Akiba came in, that hastened the disciple's recovery?

UNIT 2

1. Empathy-inducing experience (see above page T-28).

2a. Text study: Who should visit whom?

    i. Read the selection by Judah He-Ḥasid. Why should people go to visit invalids they may not even know? Isn't it enough to visit the sick that are our friends and relatives?

    ii. A response to this question is found in the second selection on page 34 (from the Jerusalem Talmud). There is a preference for visitors who are closely acquainted with the invalid during the early days of the illness. Can you think of some reasons for this preference? Do you think there is any connection between this thought and the notion that visitors should not see the invalid during certain hours of the day?

    iii. Nedarim 41a--whom not to visit. What modern diseases might fit in this category? Does this mean not to visit such a person at all? How is this dictum influenced by what the Rabbis said about decreasing illness by visiting?

    iv. What is the reason not to visit these people? What would you suggest as a compromise that might enable the visitor to visit but the invalid not to be embarassed? Read the Shulḥan Aruch, Yoreh De'ah 335:8 (on sourcebook page 36 or 37). Rather than staying in the anteroom, as suggested, what alternatives do we have today?

    (Possible responses: cards, phone calls, etc.)
Do these fit all the requirements?

2b. <u>Text study: What to do during the visit.</u>

Read the three texts on page 35.

After students have read the texts, ask for volunteers to role play the manner of visiting the sick that is suggested in these texts (or at least the second and third texts). Following the role play, ask students how they would feel doing these actions in the presence of someone who is sick. Do these suggestions help or make more difficult the role of the visitor when he enters the sickroom?

Have students attempt other possiblities of how to spend the time, consider topics of conversation, etc.

ii. Read the Shulḥan Aruch passages dealing with the sick. What new ideas are included? What are the ideas we have already learned about? Why does Shulḥan Aruch repeat what we already know?

Notes on the Shulḥan Aruch:

The Shulḥan Aruch is a law code written by Joseph Karo. Its name means "a set table" and it was written to help the masses of the Jewish people understand what was considered by the authorities of the mid-16th century to be proper halachic practice. It is a digest of Jewish law, generally presenting the conclusions of halachic discussions but not the arguments that led to the conclusions.

Karo was a Sephardic Jew (i.e., from the Mediterranean basin). After he wrote his code, a rabbi by the name of Moses Isserles wrote comments on each section where the customs of the Ashkenazic community (i.e., Jews living in Eastern Europe) differed from those of the Sephardim. As a result, the Shulḥan Aruch together with the notes by Isserles reflected Jewish law as it was practiced in all of the then-known Jewish world (excluding Chinese, Indian, and Yemenite Jewish communities).

(Adapted from Elliot Dorff, *Conservative Judaism: Our Ancestors to Our Descendants.*)

UNIT 3

1. Discussion: The involvement of the Jewish community in sick care.

   a. Ask students to read the selection on page 38 about the work of the Bikkur Ḥolim Society in the Middle Ages, as a communal sick care organization.

   b. Ask students to compare sick care in the Middle Ages (as portrayed in the article) with that of 20th century America. What kinds of health care are available today that were not in existence five hundred years ago? (Hospitals, health-related facilities, nursing and convalescent homes, pharmaceuticals, artificial limbs, mechanized wheel chairs, etc.)

   c. Ask students if they have ever heard of a Bikkur Ḥolim Society in modern times. If they have not, explain to them that in most Jewish communities, there is a group that may not be called the Ḥevrat Bikkur Ḥolim, but nevertheless does some of the same work as the traditional Society. Sometimes these groups are called "Guardians of the Ill." Who *does* visit the sick in modern times? (Rabbis.) Why do you think they do this work? If you were sick, would you want to be visited only by people whose "jobs" were to visit the sick-- or by other people who visited for other reasons as well?

   d. This would be an appropriate time for the rabbi or Jewish chaplain of the local hospital to visit and discuss the kind of work he does, helping patients. Ask him to discuss with the group the kinds of problems he and others face in this work, and the kinds of emotional difficulties that must be confronted when they come face-to-face with people who are seriously ill. The rabbi might want to discourage students from visiting those who are seriously ill. Listen to what he has to say and let the group be guided by his experience.

   e. Discuss with students how they feel about forming a Bikkur Ḥolim Society or being members of one. Are they hesitant? What are their fears?

KEY QUESTION: We have learned about how important Jewish
tradition considers visiting the sick to be. Is it enough
just to learn about it? Does having the knowledge mean that
we should act upon it? Discuss what the class could do to
actualize the ideas they have learned.

f. Review the list of illnesses (that the students compiled
    at the beginning of the unit) and the various kinds of
    care they require. What kinds of patients would the
    group most want to be involved with? (I.e., physically
    ill; those who are probably going to recover; handicapped;
    those who are at home; etc.)

g. Begin to prepare a chart that indicates the different kinds
    of responsibilities students in the group would be willing
    to take and the kinds of hospitals or health care facilities
    that should be investigated to meet the interests and abil-
    ities of the students in working with the sick. Assign
    small groups of students to gather information about local
    facilities in order to ascertain their interests in having
    a group of high school students regularly visit their
    patients.

2. Forming a Ḥevrat Bikkur Ḥolim and writing its
constitution.

a. Write a constitution for the Ḥevrah that includes
when the visits will take place, where participants
will visit, what kinds of things they ought to be prepared
to say and do as visitors; how transportation will be
worked out; who will visit together, etc. (Discourage
students from going alone; if a pair visits together,
they can discuss their experiences and problems together
and encourage each other to speak up in class sessions
about problems they have encountered.)

b. At the end of the study program, hold a party in
honor of the Ḥevrah members. Their families and friends
could be invited, depending on the wishes of the members.
(Refer to the chapter on Ḥachnasat Orḥim for advice on
how to extend invitations and how to treat guests.)

At that time, encourage students to review the texts
they learned earlier and to react to them out of their
new experience of being Ḥevrah members. (Some of the
texts are reprinted in the Appendix with space allowed
for student interpretation and comments based on their
personal experiences.)

Decide if the Ḥevrah will continue its work next year.

RESPECT FOR THE ELDERLY--HIDDUR P'NAY ZAKEN--הִדּוּר פְּנֵי זָקֵן

This chapter about Jewish attitudes toward the elderly is divided into three units. As a result of participating in this study program, students should be able to

Unit 1

1. analyze the meaning of "Love your neighbor as yourself" with regard to the elderly;

2. list a number of the needs of the elderly;

Unit 2

3. define the (traditional) terms זָקֵן (old) and שֵׂיבָה (aged) and determine if there are similar differentiations in modern times;

4. list biblical and rabbinic ideas about old age and compare them to their own ideas;

Unit 3

5. support a position on a contemporary issue dealing with old age with ideas from biblical and rabbinic literature;

6. analyze a number of problems the elderly face today that they may not have faced in the past;

7. design and carry out projects of interaction with the elderly of their community.

A background article relating problems and issues as well as traditional Jewish concerns for the elderly prefaces this chapter in the *Advisor's/Teacher's Edition*. A portion of the article introduces the student's material as well.

[The following article is from *A Guide to Aging Programs for Synagogues* (New York: The Synagogue Council of America, 1975), pp. 5-9.]

"A RATIONALE FOR SYNAGOGUE PROGRAMMING WITH THE JEWISH AGING"

WHO ARE THE JEWISH ELDERLY?

The Jewish elderly are the invisible members of the Jewish community. They very often inhabit a world seldom seen by young people or even the middle-aged. Some live in a kind of splendid isolation in the balmy climates of Florida, Arizona, and California. Many others live in far less glamorous "retirement communities" — inner-city tenements, low-income city and county housing projects, Jewish homes for the aging, and public or private nursing homes. This "invisible" portion of the Jewish community aged 65 and over is not only a substantial segment of the Jewish population of the United States — 12 per cent — but it is growing very rapidly. By 1990 it will increase by 40 per cent. By comparison, persons 65 or over today make up ten per cent of all Americans.

We know some alarming facts about the aging Jewish population in general. Forty-four per cent report annual incomes under $4,000, while only eight per cent report yearly incomes of $20,000 or above. Of all Jews between the ages 65-69, 56 per cent are women; between the ages of 70-79 this percentage grows to 58 per cent. Only seven per cent of our aged live with their children or grandchildren, while a striking 40 percent of those over 70 live alone.

A predictable, yet noteworthy, transition is also occurring. Eighty-six per cent of the Jews aged 80 or over are foreign born; but among those aged 65-69, most are native born.

The rather arbitrary grouping "over 65" includes the widest variety of people. There are the "young" elderly — a great many of whom work, do extensive volunteer service, travel, and live as actively as when they were "young" — and there are the physically infirm who cannot work or move around easily, and who are often isolated in their homes or confined to nursing homes. As with any other age group, there is a wide diversity in health, education, housing, income, religious attitudes and behavior, mental outlook, family status, and geographic location.

WHAT DOES IT MEAN TO BE OLD?

Old age means different things to different people. The way in which a particular older person copes with and reacts to this phase of his life will be related to his life experiences. The adjusted, confident, active and involved middle - aged person will bring those characteristics with him in his old age. There are, however, conditions generally associated with old age which by their very nature will affect him. Becoming old is a transition period during which all men and women face real and often disruptive changes to which they must adapt.

Change in Role. Forced retirement requires men and women to give up the work role which has been the focus of their daily activity for the major portion of their lives. Although their skills and physical ability to perform may be unchanged, they are separated from the mainstream of society, forced to accept a reduction in income, and are viewed as "dependents." This role shift often requires the adoption of an entirely new life-style and is accompanied by loss of self-esteem.

Change in Physical Capability. Age-associated health losses, including visual and hearing impairments, reduced mobility, and declining physical endurance, are real and anxiety-provoking. They estrange an invidual from his immediate physical environment, and, in a society which values strength and vigor, from other people as well. Failing health is an embarrassment which may limit the individual's desire to form new friendships or engage in activities.

Change in Self-Image. "Old" is an adjective which is difficult to ascribe to oneself. Men and women often reject the fact of their own body changes and may be reluctant to confirm their age status through association with groups of older people. (To the extent that this reluctance indicates a refusal to accept the negative societal stereotypes of the aged, it also has positive aspects.)

Change in Needs. Patterns of socialization are frequently altered by the multiple losses of role, status, income and health. They are further affected by loss of spouse, family, neighbors and friends through death or migration. An older person may find himself isolated at a time when the emotional support of others is needed. Fear, loneliness and enforced inactivity reduce participation in community life and increase isolation. Caught in this cycle, and unaware of existing community services which are available to help, these people are the most difficult to identify and often the neediest.

Even the healthy, energetic, older person lives in a society built for young people, and largely insensitive to his needs. Such older adults must struggle against false stereotypes that they are incapable of work, intellectual growth, and creative enjoyment of leisure time. The fact is that for the vast majority of older persons, only a minimum of supportive services is needed for them to maintain their independence and vitality.

THE PLACE OF THE OLDER JEW IN JEWISH CULTURE

The Jewish View of Old Age

In Jewish tradition it is not only said that we must honor our elders, but that it is an honor to achieve a ripe old age. Advanced years in themselves are not an honor, but when achieved "in the way of righteousness," "the hoary head is a crown of glory." (Proverbs 16:31)

The Bible emphasizes the inter-relationship between the way in which we live our lives, and the nature of the "harvest" of old age. The Fifth Commandment states: "Honor your father and your mother, that your days may be long in the land that the Lord thy God gives to you." And the belief that longevity is the reward for a good life is summed up in Jacob's response to the Pharaoh's question asking Jacob's age. He answered: "The days of the years of my sojournings are a hundred and thirty years; few and evil have been the days of the years of my life, and they have not attained unto the days of the years of the life of my fathers in the days of their sojournings." (Genesis 47:9)

The rabbinic literature offers a poignant counterpoint between the growth in wisdom and learning that is achievable only with age, and the physical decline characteristic of old age. "He who learns from the young, eats unripe grapes and drinks new wine," it is stated in the Talmud; while "he who learns from the old eats ripe grapes and drinks old wine." Another rabbinic sage advised: "If the old say 'tear down' and the children 'build' — tear down, for the 'destruction' of the old is construction; the 'construction' of the young, destruction." As for the physical realities, the unattractiveness of old age is treated metaphorically: "Youth is a crown of roses; old age a crown of (heavy) willows;" and practically: a man must pray that in his later years, "his eyes may see, his mouth eat, his legs walk, for in old age all powers fail."

According to the rabbis too, oldness itself is not a virtue; wisdom and knowledge of Torah determine its value. The truly successful life is one which goes on growing and developing to the very end, which reaches its last day with full mental and physical powers. (Deut. 34:7)

The Impact of Modern Society on Traditional Patterns

The traditional Jewish view of old age has been challenged by modern thought and modern lifestyles. One measure of this development can be found in contrasting the cultural patterns of European and Oriental Jews in Israel. Among the Oriental families, the tradition of veneration for the aged has persisted and nearly two-thirds of the aged live with their children, compared with about one-third of the aged of European families. In America, the early twentieth-century Jewish immigrant needed his clan. His cultural and business survival involved the extended family. However, the structure of the Jewish family and the place and esteem of the aged parent have changed with the aging of second and third generation Jewish Americans. A number of factors are involved:

1. *The Conflicting Attitudes of First Generation Jews Toward Their Parents.* Native born Jewish Americans found themselves astride a cultural conflict between the lifestyle and traditions of their immigrant parents and the cultural environment in America which was open to them. Striving for social acceptance, and working for economic success, "escape" from the old-world image into modern society carried with it an element of what a noted psychiatrist called "elder-rejection." In some cases, this elder-rejection became manifest in the relationships between the native born generation and immigrant parents. Often it was repressed and has affected the successful adjustment of the child to his own aging, for when this attitude does emerge, its focus tends to be inward: self-derogatory and self-rejecting.

2. *The Cult of Youth in American Society.* In contrast to Biblical and Middle Eastern society where it would not be uncommon for someone to exaggerate his age, few Americans over thirty can discuss their own age without embarrassment or understatement. Youthful appearance is a highly valued characteristic, and much time and money is spent cultivating this image. Gray hairs are dyed, bald heads receive toupees or transplants, faces are lifted, bodies are massaged and held together by undergarments and tight-fitting clothes. In the business and professional world, age is often a negative factor. Forced retirement is based not on loss of skills or health impairments, but on strict chronology. Hiring and promotion policies discriminate on the basis of age. Although recent legislation has been enacted which prohibits age discrimination in job hiring, the law has been of little benefit to persons over the age of 65 who wish to qualify for social security benefits.

Staying young is such an obsession that many euphemisms have been adopted simply to avoid saying "old." As the late Rabbi A.J. Heschel stated:

"A vast amount of human misery, as well as enormous cultural and spiritual damage, are due to these twin phenomena of our civilization: the contempt for the old and the traumatic fear of getting old. Monotheism has acquired a new meaning; the one and only thing that counts is being young. Youth is our god, and being young is divine. To be sure, youth is a very marvelous thing. However, the cult of youth is idolatry. Abraham is the grand old man, but the legend of Faust is pagan."

3. *Inattention to the Spiritual Life.* While the traditional Jewish society emphasized ritual, celebration, and the art of inner devotion, modern society has severed the transcendant connections implicit in our everyday lives. Preoccupation with work, productivity, and the public life have left the private, spiritual development of the inner-person relatively undeveloped. The lack of inner spiritual development, and the lack of development of a meaningful private life of study and celebration fills us with a dread of retirement from the work society and its social auxiliaries.

"Only very few people," writes Rabbi Heschel, "realize that it is in the days of our youth that we prepare ourselves for old age ... The ancient equation of old age and wisdom is far from being a misconception. However, age is no guarantee for wisdom. A Hebrew proverb maintains: 'A wise old man, the older he gets the wiser he becomes, a vulgar old man, the older he gets the less wise he becomes.' People are anxious to save up financial means for old age; they should also be anxious to prepare a spiritual income for old age. The ancient principle — listen to the voice of the old — becomes meaningless when the old have nothing meaningful to say. Wisdom, maturity, tranquility do not come all of a sudden when we retire from business."

4. *The Independence and Mobility of Nuclear Family Units.* When an older person maintained his or her position of respect as head of the family, the problems of physical decline in old age or the pain caused by the death of one's beloved were eased by family support mechanisms. Today there is a widespread pattern of elderly nuclear family units, and of older Jews dwelling alone. Many are, no doubt, estranged from their children for personal reasons; in many cases the parent or the adult child, or both, wish to maintain their own independence. The child does not want the burden of taking care of the parent and the parent does not want to "interfere" with the child's established family life, or to be dependent. At one extreme we find lonely and isolated Jewish poor, spending their later years in tenements in declining neighborhoods of the inner city, or in apartments in areas undergoing cultural transition in the fringe-city. Their children and grandchildren usually live in the suburbs, many miles away, or in another city. At the other extreme, more affluent aging Jews leave their well-to-do suburban surroundings for the peer-group environment of the retirement communities of Florida, Arizona, and California. The fact that both adult children and elderly parents *choose* to live miles from their immediate family suggests that the desire for independence, mobility, freedom, and economic advancement have become values more highly prized than the preservation of the family structure.

The attitudes of Jewish Americans of all ages toward aging and the aged are clearly in conflict with traditional Jewish values and life patterns, and represent in part a semi-conscious rejection of those values and patterns. Symptomatic relief from the ills created by the disintegration of the family structure and the neglect of inner life can be sought; but any meaningful reassertion of the traditional Jewish attitudes of veneration for the aged and contentment in old age will require a major overhaul in the educational, occupational, and residential priorities and orientations which determine the patterns of our lives.

<u>Unit 1</u>

<u>Objectives</u>:

    a. Students will be able to analyze the meaning of וְאָהַבְתָּ לְרֵעֲךָ כָּמוֹךָ with regard to the elderly.

    b. Students will be able to list a number of the needs of the elderly.

<u>Outline of Unit</u>:

1. Discussion of Proust quote.

2. Write a commentary to "Love your neighbor as yourself" that confronts the issue of the elderly.

3. Students describe elderly people with whom they are acquianted.

4. Trigger films: *To Market, To Market* and *Tagged. Shopping Bag Lady*.

5. Compare the elderly portrayed in the film and those with whom you are acquainted.

6. List the needs of the elderly (as students perceive them) today.

1. Write the Proust quote (page 46 of the sourcebook) on the blackboard. Ask students to react to it. What do they think it means? Who are the adolescents who don't last long enough? How does life make old men out of adolescents?

   Ask students if they agree with the Proust quote. Is it true that life makes old men out of adolescents who last long enough? Will life make old people out of them (the students) if they live long enough?

   Ask students if they have ever thought about growing old. What are their fears about growing old? What are some of the good things about growing old? Ask students to compare life to the voyage of a ship. How do people feel when a ship sets out on a voyage? What is the scene like on the dock? (Celebration, friends wishing safe journey, etc.) What is the scene like when the ship returns? (Usually subdued--people leaving quietly and meeting their friends, families.) When, in reality, is there greater cause for rejoicing --at the beginning or at the end of the journey? Why? (At the end: the trip has been safe and successful.) How is this like life? (We celebrate the birth of a baby--yet the future is completely unsure. As a person grows old, he may meet increasing age without celebration. Nevertheless, we ought to rejoice in the safe and wonderful passage of life. With age, people can see their accomplishments, their families grown, their dreams coming to fruition.) See the Shemot Rabbah quotation.

2. Ask students how they would want to be treated when they become old. Write a commentary to "Love your neighbor as yourself" as concerns the elderly. Ask each student to fill out the exercise "Love your neighbor as yourself" when the neighbor is an elderly person. How could you treat an elderly person in the way that you would like to be treated when you are old?

3. Have students describe elderly people with whom they are acquainted. Give participants a few minutes to "list the names of some elderly people" on page 46, and to fill in the other information. Ask each student to describe to the rest of the group, at least one of the people listed. Ask how the person's being elderly influences the student's relationship to him.

4. Trigger films: *To Market, To Market* and *Tagged*. Screen these two short films (6 minutes total) that portray a number of contemporary problems facing the elderly. Available from Jewish Media Service, 15 E. 26th St., New York, NY 10010. Another excellent film is *The Shopping Bag Lady* (20 minutes; color) available from The New York Public Library, among other resource centers.

5. Compare the elderly portrayed in the films with those with whom you are acquainted. List students' responses on the blackboard. Ask the following questions: What are the main characteristics of the elderly portrayed in the films? How are these characteristics similar to those of the elderly you know? How are they different? What do you think accounts for the differences?

6. List the needs of the elderly (as you perceive them) today. Ask students to brainstorm a number of needs of the elderly today. List their suggestions on the blackboard. Ask students to copy the list in their sourcebooks, and to keep them in mind as the group learns about the elderly in ancient times and today.

UNIT 2

Objectives:

    a. Participants will be able to define the terms
       זָקֵן (old) and שֵׂיבָה (aged). They will determine
       if there are similar differentiations in modern
       times (and define them).

    b. Students will be able to list biblical and
       rabbinic ideas about old age and will be able
       to compare them to their own ideas.

Outline of Unit:

    1. Role play: The King (Rehoboam), the elders, and young men.

    2. Text study: Definitions of old age: numerical
       age; parents; wisdom.

    3. Contrasting texts: Job 12:12 vs. Job 32:6.
       Sanhedrin 17a vs. Sanhedrin 36b.

    4. Text study: Fears precipitated by old age.

    5. Additions to the list of needs of the elderly.

    6. Questions for speaker (next session) on "The
       elderly in our community."

UNIT 2

1. <u>Role play: The king's (Rehoboam's) choice.</u> Prior to the class session, assign roles to a number of students. The roles are: new head of government; the people he governs (3 people); the young advisors (3 people); the elders (3 people). Give each participant a card that describes a role, as follows:

<u>New head of government</u>: You are the new leader of your people. Your predecessor has just died. He was a good leader, but he had rich tastes and the people were taxed heavily to support his tastes. You want very much to be the leader, but are unsure about which policies you should follow. When you are confronted with a problem, you will consult first your predecessor's elderly advisors, and then with your friends who are younger and have grown up with you.

<u>The people</u>: You have a new leader. His predecessor taxed you heavily and made you work hard for the benefit of his government. You live in the north of the country, and he rules from the south. You want to be sure that the new leader will take your needs into account when he makes decisions about what kind of leader he will be. You know that he wants you to support his government, and so you let him know that you want some things in return for your support. Tell him that his predecessor made you work too hard and that you would like him to make life easier-- lighten the load you have carried--and then you will serve him gladly.

<u>The elders</u>: You are the advisors who had served the previous leader while he was alive, and you are still available to help the new leader, if he desires your advice. When he asks you for advice about the people's request that he lighten their work load, answer him by saying something like this: "Although you are the leader, you must also be a servant to these people--you are in charge to serve their needs as well as your own. If you speak to them kindly, they will serve you faithfully."

<u>The young advisors</u>: You have grown up with the new leader. When he asks you for advice about how to answer the people, answer him by saying something like this: "Tell the people, 'If you think my predecessor treated you harshly and made you do hard work, you have no idea how you will have to work in the future! You will work harder than ever before. My predecessor was gentle in comparison to how I will be.'"

Instruct the leader to start the role play with a discussion with the people. Stop the role play after the leader has consulted the young men.

Ask students to read an account of a historical event with similar components (the story of King Rehoboam), found on page 47. Tell them to fill in the choices and answer the question at the bottom of the page.

Discuss their responses. If they think the young men gave the best advice, note the historical realities that resulted from their advice. Read (or summarize) the continuation of the I Kings 12 passage (page 48) that shows the split of the kingdom into Judah and Israel, and subsequent diminution of Rehoboam's power. Point out that this resulted from his following the advice of the young men. If they think Rehoboam should have listened to the elders, why do they think so? What made the elders' advice more reasonable? Was it related to their age?

2. <u>Text study: Defining old age and attitudes about it.</u>

Ask students to read the text of Leviticus 19:32. What
does the text instruct us to do? Why do you think it gives
these instructions? Does it make sense for us today to rise
before the old? If we did, what would we be saying about
our attitudes toward the elderly? Ask students if they
think there is a difference between the old (zaken) and
the aged (sevah).

Read the text of Avot 5:24. According to the text, is
there a difference between zaken and sevah? What is
the difference?

Ask students to refer to their notes about elderly people
they are acquainted with (page 46). Ask them to label
those who are 60-69 as "zaken" and those who are 70 or
above as "sevah."

Ask students how many of their elderly acquaintances are
over 70. Ask if they consider people over 60 to be elderly.
(They may consider people over 30 to be elderly!) Explain
to students that in ancient times, people did not live as
long on the average as we do today. A person who was for-
tunate to live to be 60 or 70 was quite a rarity. Do we
consider it unusual for people to live to be 60 or 70?
What is an age we might consider to be unusually old? How
shall we define the group of people we call "elderly"? You
may find the chart on page 50 an interesting aid.

Explain to students that the respect for the elderly that
Leviticus 19:32 teaches us is related, at least in the
ancient world, to the idea of "Honor your father and mother."
Discuss how these two ideas might be related. Take into
account the idea that if people died at earlier ages in
ancient times, then old age came on at a relatively earlier
time than we think of it today. Ask students if they consider their parents to be elderly. How is the respect they
give to their parents different from the respect demanded
in Leviticus for the elderly? How is it the same? What do
they think are the characteristics of being parents and of
being old that are the same?

3. <u>Contrasting texts: Job; Sanhedrin.</u>

Divide students into four groups, assigning each group one
of the passages on page 52 (Job or Sanhedrin). Assign the
groups the following tasks:

    Read the text you have been assigned.

    Discuss what the text means to you.

    Brainstorm as many reasons as you can that would
        support the text.

After a few minutes, reconvene the class as a whole and ask
for a representative from each group to report on the work
of his group. Ask students to try to solve this problem:

    How could the author of the Book of Job believe in
        both of these ideas?

    How could the editor of the Talmud allow both of
        these ideas to stand in one book?

Ask students to consider how each verse might refer to
different situations or circumstances. Why do you think
Jewish tradition shows such ambivalence toward the
treatment of the elderly?

    (We have already seen some differentiation between
    zaken and sevah. The tradition is well aware
    that different people age in different ways, with
    differing abilities and disabilities. Perhaps the
    tradition is advising us to treat every individual
    according to his needs and capabilities--the way
    each of us would like to be treated.)

Does anything we have read in Job or Sanhedrin in any way
modify the ideas found in Leviticus, Kiddushin, or Sefer
HaHinuch--that the elderly deserve respect because they
are wise in their own experience?

4. Text study.

Ask students to read the text from Kiddushin 32b. What do
the elderly possess that should entitle them to the respect
of younger people? Ask students if they agree with Issi
ben Yehuda when he says that we should rise before the
aged, regardless of whether or not they are learned in
the Torah. What do all elderly people have, according
to Issi ben Yehuda?

If Issi ben Yehuda had been present when Rehoboam had to
decide how to answer the people of Israel, what would he
have advised Rehoboam to do?

Does this mean that elders are always right? What is the
biblical text trying to teach in the Rehoboam story
regarding the relationship of elders and young people?

How does this relate to the teaching of Kiddushin 32b?

Read the selection from Sefer HaḤinuch. What does this
text add to the text from the Talmud in Kiddushin 32b?

4. Text study: Fear precipitated by old age.

    Read the texts on pages 54-55 one at a time. After reading
    each one, ask the question, "What problem of old age does
    this relate to?"

    When reading Avot 4:25, consider the pros and cons of writing
    on blotted-out paper. Explain the artistic notion of penti-
    mento, whereby an artist paints over what he previously painted.
    Sometimes, when we look at a painting, we can see what was
    painted underneath, on the artist's first attempt. When you
    write or paint on blotted-out paper, how does the original
    writing or drawing effect the later work?

        (The first experience may lend expertise to the second.
         Increasing experience may increase the quality of the
         writing or painting.)

    Some of the problems of old age that the texts refer to follow:

     Numbers 8: Lack of meaningful work; not part of the labor force.
     Isaiah 3: Weakness, inability to take care of oneself
     Psalm 71: Uselessness to society; becoming a burden on others
                who might resent having to help.
     Ecclesiastes 11: Physical changes (hair, strength).
     Tanḥuma: Increasing difficulty with bodily functions.
     Shir HaShirim Rabbah: Sadness that life is nearing its end.

    Note that these texts describe the problems of old age in an
    attempt to prevent abuse of the elderly. Ask students to list
    Joys of Old Age at the bottom of page 55.

5. Ask students to make any additions they feel necessary to their
    lists of the needs of the elderly on page 46.

6. Discuss the possibility of inviting someone who works with the
    elderly in your community to speak to the group about the
    problems of the elderly and the problems younger people have
    in working with them. If students would like to invite such a
    person, discuss who should be invited [see the Hachnasat Orḥim
    chapter for extending the invitation] and how long he should
    be expected to speak. Ask students to write questions to ask
    the guest speaker (on page 59). (This can be done at home if
    there is no time in class.)

The following excerpt is from Joseph L. Freedman,
בנערינו ובזקננו נלך: *Living and Learning with the Aged*
(New York: Leaders Training fellowship, 1975):

We can now try to understand why any <u>zaken</u> is deserving of
honor, even if he be a non-Jew, or even if he be a senile
old man who passes through the room never to be encountered
again. Because the <u>zaken</u> has lived so many years, it is so
many years in which he has been living in God's world.
Throughout his life every <u>zaken</u> has acquired a unique set of
experiences, a unique unfolding of the image of God within
him. By virtue of his age the <u>zaken</u> has had an opportunity
to live his life more fully than people younger than him.
By honoring the aged we come to "fear God"; i.e. we can stand
in awe of the wonder of life, its complexities, ecstacies and
disappointments, potential for good as well as for evil, as
exemplified by the life of the <u>zaken</u>. Even if we are repulsed
by a particular <u>zaken</u>'s appearance, personality, or senility,
we have a positive commandment not only to look beyond the
externals and to honor him for having lived in the universe, but
also to look up to the <u>zaken</u> as a potential role model. We can
learn from the <u>zaken</u>, whether brilliant or senile, vegetating
or robust. We can place ourselves positively in his shoes and
say, "How can I live up to my own potential so that when I am
as old as he I will be able to look back at a full and satisfying life?" We do not look at what the old person has
produced in his or her life, but rather we look at the life
which the old person has lived. By so honoring the aged,
aging itself becomes not a dreaded eventuality, but an aim
and guiding force throughout our lives. The whole process of
aging becomes worthwhile....Instead of feeling shunned and
discarded, the <u>z'kenim</u> themselves will be able to feel that
they are needed, that until they die they are fulfilling vital
roles in society. Professor Abraham J. Heschel, <u>zikhrono
livrakha</u>, summarized the ramifications of the performance of
this important mitzva:

> We must seek ways to overcome the traumatic fear
> of being old, the prejudice, the discrimination
> against those advanced in years. All men are
> created equal, including those advanced in years.
> Being old is not necessarily the same as being
> stale. The effort to restore the dignity of
> old age will depend upon our ability to revive
> the equation of old age with wisdom. Wisdom is
> the substance upon which the inner security of
> old age will forever depend. But the attain-
> ment of wisdom is the work of a lifetime. (from
> "To Grow in Wisdom" in *The Insecurity of Freedom)*

Unit 3

Objectives:

a. Students will be able to support a position on a contemporary legal issue dealing with old age with ideas from biblical and rabbinic literature.

b. Students will be able to analyze a number of problems the elderly face today that they did not face when they were younger.

c. Students will be able to design and carry out projects of interaction with the elderly of their community.

Outline of the Unit:

1. Debate a current legal issue, utilizing texts from Jewish tradition for support.

2. Speaker: The elderly in our community.

3. Additions to list of needs of the elderly.

4. List rules for treatment of the elderly.

5. Planning projects.

UNIT 3

1. <u>Debate a current legal issue (concerning the elderly)
    utilizing texts from Jewish tradition for support.</u>
    Suggested topic: mandatory retirement.

    Ask students to read the introductory material about
    the issue on pages 56-57.

    Let students go to parts of the room designated for

            a. Those favoring mandatory retirement at age 65;

            b. Those opposing mandatory retirement at age 65
                (i.e., those favoring a later age);

            c. Those opposing mandatory retirement (at any age).

    Allow students about five minutes to decide on which
    texts from Jewish tradition they will use to support their
    point of view.

    Start the debate by stating the issue and asking the side
    which favors retirement at age 65 to explain its position.
    Allow equal time for each of the other viewpoints to ex-
    plain its position. Allow each side to ask questions of
    the others, which representatives will have to respond to.

    The debate should not last longer than 25-30 minutes.
    Ask each side to summarize the arguments of the opposing
    sides.

    Spend a few minutes debriefing the debate and discussing
    what attitudes toward age and the elderly were exposed
    during the debate.

Additional background information for discussion leaders:
"Reprinted from 'U.S. News & World Report,'" (October 3, 1977)

BIG FIGHT OVER RETIREMENT AT AGE 65

Millions of people, young as well as old, will feel the impact of a legislative drive to outlaw mandatory retirement before age 70.

Businessmen and their employes soon may be adjusting themselves to this new circumstance: People cannot be forced to leave their jobs at age 65.

Despite a clear trend in many industries and occupations toward early retirement, Congress seems likely to pass legislation that would, in effect, outlaw mandatory retirement before age 70 for most workers. The House passed such a bill on September 23 by a 359-to-4 vote. Its version also prohibits forced retirement within the Federal Government at any age.

Edge of the wedge. Many legislators in Washington see the forthcoming law as the entering wedge toward abolishing compulsory retirement entirely in private industry. Says Representative Paul Findley (Rep.), of Illinois: "Mandatory retirement will be outlawed. This bill is just a step toward that goal."

Even the first step, should it become law, will have an impact on employment practices of U.S. businesses and upon the lives of many workers:

• The size of the nation's work force will grow and so, in all likelihood, will unemployment.

• Pension plans that contain mandatory-retirement dates will need to be renegotiated by union and management representatives.

• The financial burden on the Social Security system will be eased a bit as some workers stay on the job longer.

• Younger people may have to wait longer for promotions because those ahead of them will not be moving out as fast.

• Some businesses may decide to fire marginal workers in mid-career rather than letting them stay on until age 70.

The long-term impact of the pending legislation is far from clear. Will corporations need to devise objective standards for deciding which older workers can no longer perform their duties effectively? Will attitudes of people change as a result of the law, causing larger numbers of people to work beyond 65? Will executives be prone to stay on the job longer than those in subordinate positions do?

"We're about to make a major change in the structure of industry, and nobody is sure what will happen as a result," says one key Government official who is involved in Administration discussions of the proposed law. "You can construct completely opposite scenarios—that older workers will be helped or hurt, that the economy will benefit or suffer."

According to the Economic Unit of *U.S. News & World Report,* about 25 per cent of the nation's 91 million workers are subject to mandatory retirement at age 65 because of company rules. If 1 of every 4 persons facing mandatory retirement in the next five years were to continue working past age 65, some 600,000 to 650,000 older workers would be added to the labor force—an average of about 125,000 per year.

The impact of these additional workers on the nation's unemployment rate, other things being equal, would be to raise it slightly more than one tenth of a percentage point each year, or six tenths of a percentage point over five years, says a study by the Economic Unit. The unemployment rate is presently 7.1 per cent of the labor force.

If the age of forced retirement is raised to 70, no further growth of unemployment would be likely after five years, since by then a normal retirement cycle would have resumed.

On the other hand, the labor force has grown by 2.3 million persons in the last 12 months, and 2.9 million additional jobs were added to the economy. Proponents of ending age bias on the job cite such figures in arguing that the pending bill will not glut the labor market with many more workers than it can handle.

Some estimates of how the proposed law would affect the labor market suggest a large jump in unemployment. Sears, Roebuck & Company surveyed its own employes, then projected the findings to include the country's total labor force. The company discovered that one third of its nonmanagement employes would work past age 65 if the firm's mandatory-retirement age were raised by law to 70.

Applying that same ratio to the entire economy, Sears predicted that the proposed law would raise unemployment by one half of 1 percentage point next year, and by 1 percentage point by 1982. Sears said that its own hiring of new workers would be reduced by 7 per cent, and that promotions below the management level in the company would decrease 8.3 per cent. The company gave its study wide distribution among Congressmen and Administration officials in a move to hold back enactment of the pending bill.

If later retirements prevented jobs from opening up, young workers would find their job opportunities stunted, some businessmen complain. "If legislation is passed to eliminate mandatory retirement, a slowdown in turnover within the work force, with increased unemployment, will follow automatically," says Arthur C. Prine, Jr., vice president of R. R. Donnelley & Sons. "And we know that the major impact of unemployment unfortunately falls on younger and minority workers."

But testimony in the House by corporate executives opposed to raising the mandatory-retirement age disclosed few fears that large numbers of workers would refuse to retire at 65. "Our experience," said George B. Morris of General Motors Corporation, "would indicate that a mandatory-retirement age is more or less academic. People are not staying that long. People are retiring earlier and earlier every year."

GM's retirement age for hourly paid workers is 68. But only 2 per cent of the workers last year—in a company employing 450,000 production workers—are waiting till age 68 to retire. The experience of other big corporations with pension plans permitting early retirement is similar.

Few over 65. Inland Steel Company, whose contract with the United Steelworkers of America bans forced retirement, notes that just 41 out of 18,243 production workers at its mill near Chicago are over age 65.

But for the minority of workers who relish the income or enjoyment of their jobs, retirement at any age seems absurd. Says William H. Hightower, Jr., board chairman of Thomaston Mills in Georgia: "I can tell you this: I'm in my 66th year, and I'm not about to retire—to hell with Social Security." Or, as 77-

year-old Representative Claude Pepper (Dem.), of Florida, says, "Some people dodder at 30, others at 80, and some pass through life without doddering at all."

Even so, many executives complain they will be hard-pressed to make a fair determination about whether employes who want to work past 65 are physically and mentally competent to do so.

Henry J. Lartigue, Jr., manager of employe relations for Exxon Company, USA, puts the problem this way: "If an individual said, 'I don't want to retire,' then the company would have to make a judgment that he was not able to work effectively. That would cause disputes and problems between the company and employes. It would cause grievances and more concerns and pose more potential discrimination than a policy that is uniform for all. It would disrupt the orderly system that has really worked and served our employes very well."

Removal of deadwood. For some companies, the answer may be to clear out deadwood amid the ranks of workers by dismissing, even before normal retirement age, those whose work is unsatisfactory. Out of fear that a worker will hang onto a job far past age 65, the boss might fire him or her at age 55 instead.

But some executives of companies with no mandatory-retirement age assert that they have encountered few management nightmares of that sort. "It seems that the older employe is among the first to realize when the job is suffering," says Gerald L. Maguire, of Bankers Life & Casualty Company. "If it looks like the person can do the job, we still hire people 55 or 70 years old—but it has to be on the basis of ability." Maguire's own boss, Chairman John D. MacArthur, is 80.

The new law could relieve financial pressure on the Social Security system. For several years, contributions to the system would be higher, and payouts to retirees lower, than presently planned, because people who otherwise would have begun receiving benefits at age 65 would continue working a while longer. The same holds true for private pension plans. Health-insurance costs of companies would be little affected, since at age 65 medicare assumes most of the cost of health-care payments once financed by employers.

As a political issue, mandatory retirement is a relative newcomer. When the Social Security Act took effect four decades ago, age 65 was set as the time of eligibility for full benefits—but retirement then or at any other age was never made mandatory. Forced retirement was written into many private pension plans begun after World War II.

For management, this was a tool for gracefully getting rid of older workers whose output had declined. For unions, few of whose blue-collar members wished to work past 65 anyway, it was an easy way to cope with unemployment among younger workers.

As years went by, the benefits of private pension plans were beefed up, and pensions were made available at earlier and earlier ages.

An auto worker, for example, now can retire at any age with a $650-a-month pension after 30 years of work. In 1972, for the first time, a majority of all Social Security retirement checks went to early retirees.

In response to complaints that older workers of all ages were being unfairly treated in the business world, Congress in 1967 passed the Age Discrimination in Employment Act banning job-related bias against persons between the ages of 40 and 65. Most private employers of more than 20 persons are covered by that legislation, and so are all levels of government.

Efforts in Congress to raise or eliminate the age ceiling in the law began about four years ago. Each year, more and more lawmakers signed on as co-sponsors, until the number reached 115 in the House. Extensive hearings were held last March. Yet, few people thought the legislation would clear Congress any time soon.

When the bill came to the House floor for debate on September 13, the only dissenting voice was that of Representative John N. Erlenborn (Rep.), of Illinois. He urged that the effective date be made two years after enactment instead of six months afterward. "At least," he said, "we can have second thoughts about it before it takes effect."

"Tremendous pressure." Caught off guard, many business groups and corporations opposed to the bill concentrated their lobbying efforts on the Senate, where a vote has not been scheduled. "Business is putting a tremendous amount of pressure on now," said a staff member of the Senate Human Resources Committee. Joining the corporations in fighting the bill were many colleges and universities, which claimed that mandatory retirement is the only practical way of getting rid of tenured professors. The AFL-CIO, opposed to mandatory retirement but unhappy that the legislation would interfere with the negotiated pension plans now requiring it, took little part in the debate.

Few congressional sources give opponents much chance of stopping the bill from reaching President Carter's desk by some time next year, at the latest. And few observers doubt that the President will sign it.

[The bill to extend the age of mandatory retirement from 65 to 70 was passed by the U.S. Congress in October, 1977.]

(Unit 3, Continued)

2. Speaker: The elderly in our community.

    Ask the speaker to spend a few minutes discussing general
    problems of the elderly in the community. The majority
    of the time should be spent responding to the students'
    questions. Ask students to note the speaker's responses
    and to comment on them on page 59.

3. Additions to the list of needs of the elderly.

    Ask students to turn back to page 46 and add any new
    thoughts they have had about the needs of the elderly.

4. List rules for treatment of the elderly.

    Assign students to work in small groups to develop a set
    of rules for how to treat the elderly.

    Situations that should be considered include

        a. treatment of elderly relatives;

        b. treatment of the elderly in a public situation
            (where the students do not know the elderly
            person);

        c. treatment of the elderly in a social or
            "helping" context.

    Ask the groups to share their lists with each other and
    to come to some consensus on issues of contention.

    Compile a complete list, taking into account the sug-
    gestions of all of the groups. (After students complete
    a project of working with the elderly, ask them to review
    the lists and to modify them, as necessary.)

5. <u>Planning projects.</u>

Students should have a few days to reflect on the work they have done before entering the "Project Planning" stage.

Ask students to answer the questions on the bottom of page 67 prior to discussing what projects they could undertake to help the elderly in their community.

An important point that should emerge from answering the questions is that both young people and the elderly can give to each other. After students have responded in writing and orally to the questions, brainstorm for ideas of projects that could be done which would demonstrate how teenagers can help the elderly and how the elderly can help teenagers.

Some suggestions:*

   a. <u>Oral History Project:</u> Students could interview the elderly in their town about what it was like to live there when the elderly were teenagers. Students would then be utilizing the wisdom and experience of the elderly to help them understand the history of their town and how it developed. Students might then plan a presentation of their findings--perhaps using pictures and other memorabilia from the old people they interview-- and invite their families and the elderly people they interviewed to be the audience. A project of this nature is fully outlined in *Oral History Project* by Rabbi James Lebeau, published by United Synagogue Youth.

   b. <u>Study together:</u> Invite elderly members of the community to study about tzorchei tzibbur with the class. It has been noted that the elderly would be well-suited and available to do acts of gemilut ḥasadim. The students of all ages could learn about these mitzvot together, and do them together, working in a cooperative relationship.

   c. <u>Grandparents' Day:</u> Students could invite (their own) grandparents to share a day of activities with them. The activities would have to be planned with sensitivity to the needs and disabilities of the individuals involved.

After students have planned a basic outline for a project with the elderly, they should consult an expert (the community worker who spoke to them or the rabbi would be a good resource) to ascertain the suitability, probability of success, and areas of potential problems, of their plans for the elderly in their community.

---

* An excellent resource for project planning with the elderly is *A Guide to Aging Programs for Synagogues* published by the Synagogue Council of America.

REDEEMING CAPTIVES--PIDYON SHEVUYIM--פִּדְיוֹן שְׁבוּיִים

Introduction

This chapter is divided into three units that deal with historical and modern problems in ransoming or saving captives.

As a result of participating in this chapter, students will be able to:

> Unit 1: List pros and cons for establishing a priority list of captives to be redeemed; list the needs of modern captives and analyze how they might be satisfied.
>
> Unit 2: List a number of historical and modern priorities established by the Jewish people for ransoming or saving captives.
>
> Unit 3: Plan and participate in a campaign to free one or more Jewish captives.

It is assumed that nothing in the students' experience even remotely approaches the notion of physical captivity and therefore no direct empathy-inducing exercises or activities are suggested.

There is, however, a possibility that the parents, relatives, or friends of some of the students have been prisoners of war or hijacking hostages. If a student has endured such a traumatic experience, he should be allowed to decide for himself whether or not he wishes to participate in this unit of study. If he chooses to study *Pidyon Shevuyim*, discuss exactly how he wants to participate. His family or friends may prove to be valuable resources to this unit of study--if he and they wish to discuss their personal experiences with the class.

(See, also, the NOTE on pages T-26, T-27.)

UNIT 1

Objectives:

a. Students should be able to list pros and cons for establishing a priority order for how to save captives.
b. Students should be able to list the needs of modern captives and analyze how they might be satisfied.

Outline of Unit:

1. Case histories of six Soviet Jewish "refuseniks."

2. Small group work: determine what the strengths and weaknesses of an individual captive are in terms of being a "candidate" for help from the class and in terms of how effective that help might be.

3. Discussion: Small group presentations. Is choosing to help only the highest priority captive a good or bad idea?

1. <u>Case histories of six Soviet Jewish "refuseniks."</u>

Have students glance at the brief case histories of six Soviet
Jews who are "refuseniks." (The case histories are printed on
pages 63-66 so that students can refer to them later in the
lesson.)

After reading the case histories, ask students why Soviet Jews
are considered to be captives. Are all Soviet Jews captives?
Are those who are sentenced to prison terms or to internal
exile captives? Are those who are refused permission to emigrate captives? Are those who do not want to emigrate and
who function as normal Soviet citizens captives?

Agree on a definition of the word "captive" in modern terms.
Ask students to suggest situations Jews have been in during
the 20th century that made them captives.
> (The definition should include the notion of being
> dependent upon the will of some power greater than
> the Jewish community. Captivity may also be de-
> fined by the desire of the captor to exact some
> payment, penalty, or recognition from those who wish
> to save the captive. Examples of 20th century
> captives:

holocaust victims	Soviet Jews
hijacking victims	South African blacks
Jews in Arab Countries	Political dissidents
	in totalitarian
	countries

Ask students to fill in information on the "Needs of Captives"
form, page 72. Explain to students that the Jewish community
has traditionally felt the need to help Jews who were captives.
Jews felt this need for a number of reasons: they believed that
every Jew was responsible for other Jews; they recognized the
possibility that they too might someday be captives of some re-
gime or another--and would want their brothers to work on their
behalf, for their freedom; they believed that captivity ultimately would result in the loss of the lives of the captives--
and Jews were willing to make great sacrifices in order to save
lives--Jewish or non-Jewish.

We face a similar situation today with the problems of Soviet
        We keep asking ourselves: What can we to to help? One
solution has been to work on behalf of individual refuseniks,
because saving all Soviet Jews may be too large a task to
accomplish--or because saving all Soviet Jews must ultimately
begin with saving each individual.

Each of the "refuseniks" you were introduced to in this chapter
is still a captive in the Soviet Union.* None of them is free
to make decisions about his own life and the lives of loved ones.
In order to help us learn more about these refuseniks, we are
going to do some work to determine what are the critical elements
of each one's situation, so that we, as a class, might be able to
make an educated and thoughtful decision about which of these
refuseniks should receive our help first. Keep in mind the
questions raised by the "Needs of Captives" form. Which of
the needs of captives can be satisfied by individuals or by
the Jewish community as a whole--and which may not be satisfied at all?

*Hopefully this will not always be the case!

2. Small group work: determine what the strengths and weaknesses of an individual captive are in terms of being a "candidate" for help from the class and in terms of how effective that help might be.

    Assign students to work in six small groups. Randomly assign each group one of the captives who was discussed in the case histories. The task of the groups is as follows:

    List those aspects of the captive's situation that make
     you think he should be saved as soon as possible.
    List any drawbacks you can see that would make you lean
     against trying to help this captive as soon as possible.
    Write a speech that will convince the rest of the class
     that the captive you have studied about is the one on
     whose behalf the class should work first.

3. Discussion: <u>Small group speech presentations. Is choosing to help only the highest priority captive (first) a good or a bad idea?</u>

    Ask a representative of each group to read the group's speech to the class.

    Tell the class that their task eventually will be to decide on <u>one</u> of the six captives to adopt as a class project--to work on behalf of one refusenik to speed up his release. Ask them how they feel about having to choose one refusenik at a time to help. Do they agree that we should concentrate our efforts and help one family at a time? What would be the advantages of trying to help all Soviet Jews? What would be the disadvantages?

    Tell the class that the issue of captivity was not always a far-removed one from the lives of those who tried to free captives. In ancient times--and even in some modern situations--Jews were confronted with the horrible experience of seeing their friends and relatives taken into captivity. They had to decide how to go about saving them. Generally, saving them meant ransoming them--paying money in order to insure their safe release. Inasmuch as few people and communities had enough money to ransom many captives, the issue of establishing a list of priorities--who to help first--was a personal and perplexing one. During the next session, we will take a look at how the Rabbis of the Talmud and of the Middle Ages viewed their responsibility for ransoming captives--and how they chose to order their priorities for effecting the ransom.

Unit 2

Objectives:
    a. Students should be able to list pros and cons
        for establishing a priority order for how to
        save captives;

    b. Students should be able to list a number of
        historical and modern circumstances that have
        required the ransom or saving of captives.

Outline of Unit:

    1. Text study: List of priorities for whom to
        save first (Talmud and Mishnah Torah).

    2. Text study: What should and should not be done
        in order to save captives.

    3. Compare and contrast talmudic and medieval
        and modern considerations.

1. Text study: List of priorities for whom to save first.
   (from the Talmud and the Mishnah Torah)

Ask students to read the text from Horayot 13a aloud.
Explain the inter-relationships described between oneself, one's
father, teacher, and mother, and a scholar, a king of
Israel, a High Priest, and a prophet. Use the biblical
references to help explain the reasoning and priorities
of the Rabbis.

Ask students to list the order of priority for redeeming
captives taught by Horayot 13a in the space provided on
page 73.

Ask students to read the text from Baba Kamma 117b on
on page 74. What is the special circumstance described
in the text? Does it teach something new or does it
agree with the teachings of Horayot 13a?

Give students time to discuss the questions on page 74.
Discuss their responses.

2. <u>Text study: What should and should not be done in order to save captives.</u>

Read each of the sections from the Mishnah Torah separately (pages 75-76). Ask the students to paraphrase each section.

Ask students to list on page 76 the order for redeeming captives according to Maimonides. How does this list compare with the list from Horayot? How have the historical concerns changed between the time of the Rabbis of the Talmud and Maimonides (approximately 800 years)? What historical conditions that students know about might have influenced these changes? What seems to be the basic reasoning or logic that underlies their priorities? List student responses on blackboard. Which paragraphs from the Mishnah Torah give us an idea about how important the mitzvah of redeeming captives was in medieval times?

Ask students to list on the blackboard rules about redeeming captives that Maimonides formulated other than the priority order in which to help them. Those who studied Paragraph #11 should refer to its talmudic antecedent--Baba Batra 3b (see page 77).

How are the rules about not paying more than a man's value (as a slave) and not encouraging captives to escape related?
 (Both are concerned with diminishing abuses.)

Can you think of a situation wherein helping a captive to escape would not increase abuses against other captives?
 (When the captors are holding only one captive and there are and will be no others that could be treated poorly.)

Why do you think Maimonides doesn't mention this possibility--that there might be a case when it is permissible to help a captive escape?
 (Apparently this was unlikely during his lifetime. There must have been many captives, the possibility of a captor controlling only one being very unlikely.)

Which of the rules from the Talmud and from the Mishnah Torah do you think would still be valid today? In the case of helping Soviet Jews?

3. Compare and contrast talmudic and medieval guidelines for ransoming captives with modern considerations.

Divide students into groups of 3 or 4. Assign the following task:

> We have now had an opportunity to see what the rabbis of previous generations thought Jews ought to do in order to ransom captives, as well as the order in which they thought captives ought to be ransomed.
>
> Consider what decisions must be made if two people are in imminent danger (or have the best chance of being saved). How would you determine which one to help first? Take into account the priorities of the Rabbis (in the texts on pages 73-78) as well as your own feelings when writing your list of priorities.
>
> Write a list of priorities that describes character- istics of captives or their situations that you think should be considered as requiring top priority con- sideration, next level consideration, etc. (An example of a possible top priority consideration might be a person whose life is in imminent danger, or a person who has the best chance of being saved.)

When students have completed the task, re-convene the class as a whole and ask the groups to share the pro- ducts of their discussions. Try to establish a list of priorities that reflects a consensus of the thinking of most members of the class.

Compare and contrast the class list of priorities with the list given in the Talmud. What are the areas of similarity (in principle if not also in terminology)? What are the areas of differences?

Unit 3

Objective: Students should be able to plan and
participate in a campaign to free one
or more Jewish captives.

Outline of Unit:

1. Decide who is the Soviet captive of
highest priority among the six described
in this unit.

2. Decide how the group will work: Will
everyone work to help one captive? Will
small groups work to help a number of
captives?

3. Plan a campaign to help the captive(s)
chosen by the group.

4. Conduct the campaign.

5. Evaluate immediate and long-range effects
of the campaign; should the work be
continued?

Unit 3

1. <u>Decide who is the Soviet captive of highest priority among the six described in this unit.</u>

List the class order of priorities on the blackboard. Ask students to review the cases of the six Soviet Jewish families silently. Ask students to compare the details of the cases with the issues of priority on the board. Ask students to make a personal judgment about which of the Soviet Jews ought to be helped first according to the rules which the class has written. Students can be asked to fill in the personal record-keeping sheet on page 80.

List on the board the names of the captive(s) that students think ought to be helped first. Ask students to speak on behalf of each of the possibilities, discussing the reasons for supporting each. Through this discussion, one or two individuals should emerge as the most likely to acquire the support of the group, according to the guidelines written by the group.

If more than one individual emerges as the choice from the discussion, divide the class along the lines of the individuals they are supporting and ask each group to develop the strongest argument they can, in line with the class guidelines, for why <u>their</u> Soviet captive should be the one supported by the class.

Allow a short amount of time for each group to present its argument. Try to evaluate the pros and cons of helping each captive according to the class guidelines.

If necessary, discuss the democratic need to participate even if your "candidate" wasn't selected.

If students are not satisfied to work as one large group for one captive, you may have to decide to allow different groups to work for different captives.

2. Decide how the group will work: Will everyone work to help one captive? Will small groups work to help a number of captives?

    Ask students if they want to make one group decision--about the highest priority captive--and to work on his behalf as a large group? How will some students feel if their highest priority captive is not chosen by the group? (Should you participate even if your "candidate" isn't selected?) If there are strong feelings (based on the class priorities) about working on behalf of a number of captives, discuss the advantages and disadvantages of splitting the large group into small working groups. Allow students to make the decision about how they will work.

    What are the moral problems with choosing to help one person of the six? One from among the thousands of Jews wishing to leave?

3. Plan a campaign to help the captive(s) chosen by the group.

    Information about projects and programs that can help Soviet Jews is detailed on pages 67-71 and T-69-71. Specific Soviet Jews discussed in this program also have specific problems which the group(s) can address in planning an appropriate campaign on their behalf. Refer to page 72 to review what needs of modern captives students night be able to satisfy. *Note: Soviet Jews believe that out activities on their behalf does make a difference. Many have been released because of campaigns that bring attention to their plight!*

4. Conduct the Campaign.

    Be sure that every student has a role to play in the campaign.

5. Evaluate immediate and long-range effects of the campaign. Should the work be continued, and if so, how?

    Discuss if the work on behalf of Soviet Jews worthwhile even if it "failed," if the people for whose relase students worked remain captives. Are there some needs of the captives that the work does satisfy?

(Based on material by the Greater New York Conference on Soviet
Jewry, 11 W. 42nd St., New York, N.Y. 10036.)

SOVIET JEWRY DAY

Morning Program

I. As students enter the room and chat among themselves, the
teacher should, as inconspicuously as possible, record bits of
their conversations containing Jewish references, e.g., Hebrew
words, mention of Israel, religious ritual, Jewish songs, etc.

II. Sign on class room or youth lounge should read "By Order of
the Government: Religious Serviced Forbidden." Post uniformed
guards at entrance to prayer room and direct participants to an
alternate room. If prayers are said in room, have guards enter
and post sign on blackboard. Short discussion should follow
prayers in which students are encouraged to express their
reactions to the disruption in morning routine.

III. As students settle into classes, teachers should announce
names of students "caught" using overt Jewish symbols. These
students should then be sent to some appropriate site for
"detention" to await trial.

IV. Mock Trial: Assign participants the roles of prosecutor,
witnesses, defense attorney, judge, etc. Elements of actual
Soviet trials of activists to be included are lack of substantial
evidence against defendants, refusal on part of the prosecutor
and judge to comply with legal procedures, denial of entry to
courtroom of Western newsmen and relatives of defendants,
sentencing of defendant to longer term than that requested
by prosecutor.

V. Following trial have students discuss and write about how
they imagine Jews their age manage to identify as Jews
without being permitted to wear yarmulkas, attend Jewish schools
or synagogues, eat kosher food, learn about Jewish history or
rituals, etc.

VI. Simulate the exit process.

    A. Hand out "identification papers" to each student. They
        should contain:

        --internal Soviet passport, bearing student's new
          identity as a Soviet citizen;

        --information regarding his or her profession and family;

        --short history of his/her emigration status (i.e,, how
          many times visa application was filed, was it granted or
          denied, were any close relatives permitted to leave, etc.).

> --money (to some students) for bribes, fees, or taxes;
> --special information: whether exit will be hampered by dependence of sick relatives, prior military service, access to classified information, knowledge of Hebrew, etc.;
> --specific instructions on obtaining visa;
> --map of government offices, guarded checkpoints in camp and location of "airport," "secret hiding place," "Israel," etc.

> Each set of identification papers should be different.

B. Set up the following in various locations:
--Dutch embassy (which processes invitations from Israel);
--OVIR (visa) Office;
--Bank;
--Places of business where *karakteristika*--character references--must be obtained from employers;
--Housing authority (to certify the sale or return of apartment and to arrange for necessary repairs departure).

> Post guards at each location.

C. Give students a strict deadline by which time they have to have escaped to freedom or be arrested.

D. Part of the auditorium or gymnasium could be designed as as a model "Israel," complete with Israeli music, refreshments and a Hebrew-speaking welcoming committee.

E. Following the "escape" have students discuss and write about this reenactment of the emigration process.

VII. Assign students independent research projects in which they could use the New York Times and other periodicals to examine:

--the state of religion in the U.S.S.R.;
--detente as viewed by the United States and the Soviet Union;
--recent trials of Soviet Jewish activists and the reaction by Jewish groups in the West;
--the rights guaranteed by the United States and Soviet Constitutions and the international human rights treaties, including the International Declaration of Human Rights and the Helsinki Accords.

Afternoon Programs

I. Show Soviet Jewry film or slide show.

II. Invite speaker to address assembly or individual classroom.

III. Hold a Soviet Jewry poster, slogan, song or art display contest.

IV. Stage a mock trial of U.S.S.R. for violations of international treaties, e.g., the Helsinki Accord and the International Declaration of Human Rights, specifically with regard to clauses guaranteeing reunification of families, mail delivery, telephone service, religious and cultural rights, and freedom from harrassment.

(Based on material by the Greater New York Conference on Soviet
  Jewry, 11 W. 42nd St., New York, NY 10036.)

SOVIET JEWRY FREEDOM SHABBAT

A. Invite as resource people former Soviet Jewish Prisoners of
    Conscience or refuseniks, or recent tourists to the Soviet Union.

B. Use poster, "By Order of the Government: Services Forbidden"
    for Shabbat services to heighten awareness of religious
    restrictions in the Soviet Union.

C. Recite a Soviet Jewry prayer at all services.

D. For Friday night "z'mirot" (Sabbath songs) use the Soviet
    Jewry Song Sheet with emphasis on those written by Soviet
    Jews themselves, e.g., *Or Ḥadash*.

E. Set one place setting at each table with a prisoner's photograph.

F. Focus discussion groups on Soviet Jewry themes, e.g., *Klal
    Yisrael* (community of Israel), *pidyon shevuyim* (redemption of
    the captives), etc. Of particular interest are the prisoners
    who attempt to celebrate Shabbat inside labor camp.

G. At Saturday morning services:

    --set aside a seat for a Soviet Jewish Prisoner of Conscience.
      Drape it with a tallit and, if possible, a photograph of
      that prisoner;

    --dedicate one "aliyah" to that prisoner and honor one
      student with it;

    --say a "Mi Shebayrach" prayer for all Soviet Jewish prisoners.

H. Perform dramatizations or skits.

I. After Shabbat, place phone call to a Soviet Jewish activist.

A kit of materials can be ordered from the National Conference
on Soviet Jewry or one of its local affiliates.

HONOR OF THE NEEDY--K'VOD HE'ANI--כְּבוֹד הֶעָנִי

This chapter is divided into three units that deal with
how the Jewish community has traditionally dealt with the
issue of giving money and material goods to help the poor,
and with the options available in the modern world for how
to practice this. As a result of participating in this
study program, students should be able to

> Unit 1: List examples of the way the Rabbis of
> the Talmud encouraged sensitivity to the
> needs of the poor; write a set of guide-
> lines for how to collect and distribute
> money to the poor;

> Unit 2: List examples of the way the authors of
> medieval codes of Jewish law encouraged
> sensitivity to the needs of the poor;
>
> compare and contrast their own guidelines
> with those of the authors of the codes;

> Unit 3: Evaluate contemporary methods of collecting
> and distributing money to the poor by the
> standard of traditional Jewish guidelines
> from the Talmud and codes;
>
> decide on their future involvment with
> tzedakah, and plan for future meetings
> and activities concerning tzedakah.

Instructions for "Collection"

At the end of the session that precedes the beginning
of the unit on tzedakah, ask students to read the
information about "Collection" on page 86. Randomly
assign students to work on this assignment in 1's,
2's, 3's, and 4's making the distribution into groups
of different numbers as balanced as possible. Ask
participants from each grouping to meet together in
various places in the room in order to set a time for
collecting tzedakah which is acceptable to all the
members. (If some members cannot come to an agreement
about a time to meet, make some quick switches among
the groups in order to accommodate scheduling.)

Before students leave the room, remind them that the
"Collection" assignment will be the first item on the
agenda of the next session.

UNIT 1

Objectives:

   a. Students will be able to list examples of the
      ways the Rabbis of the Talmud encouraged
      sensitivity to the needs of the poor.

   b. Students will be able to write a set of
      guidelines for how to collect and distribute
      money to the poor.

Outline of Unit:

   1. Collection. Explain and enact.

   2. De-brief "Collection," an activity students have
      done prior to class.

   3. Distribute money collected by students among
      causes supported by Tikun Olam. *
      Discuss the distribution activity, in terms
      of the task itself and of the number of
      people who participated in the task.

   4. Collection of tzedakah from students and
      discussion of elements of process.

   5. Text Study: talmudic texts that describe the
      process of collecting and distributing money.

   6. Discussion: How do the talmudic texts relate
      to the biblical verse, "Love your neighbor as
      yourself"?

   7. Write guidelines for how to collect and
      distribute money for tzedakah.

   * *USY Chapters make their contributions through the
   Tikun Olam Program, explained below.*

1. <u>Debrief "Collection," an activity students have done
   prior to class.</u>

Ask students to sit with other members of their "Collection"
groups. Students who did not participate in the "Collection"
activity, because of inability to participate, should be
divided among the groups which did the assignment so they can
benefit from the discussion of the group's experiences.

Ask group members to caucus to decide on which of their
collection experiences was most successful and which least
successful.

Representatives of each group should summarize the group's
most and least successful collecting experiences. Students
should not use the names of the people from whom they
collected in their reports. Ask members of the other
groups to react to the reports.

Are there basic principles that emerge from the various
experiences that show why some people are more hesitant to
give and others less hesitant? Is there something about
the way people are approached or who approaches them or how
many people approach them that defines whether or not
collectors will receive a donation. List students'
hypotheses about "Ideal Ways of Collecting Tzedakah."

(Note that "success" in collecting is not to be equated
 with the "ideal ways.")

Ask students how close they think this collecting
experience has been to the reality of how people
collect for charities today? What differences do
they perceive?

2. Distribute money collected by students among causes supported by Tikun Olam. (USY chapters do this through the Tikun Olam Program administered through the USY Central office.) Ask students to remain in their groups and to discuss how the money they have collected ought to be distributed. Tell them they may choose to send their money to any of the funds and institutions supported by Tikun Olam that are listed on pages 88 (89-91). Ask each group to fill in their choices as indicated on page 88, to copy their choices onto the manilla envelope into which they have deposited the money they have collected, and to give the envelopes to you.

Discuss the distribution activity, in terms of the task itself and the number of people who participated in the task.

Ask students to discuss how they felt about deciding where the money should be donated. How would they have felt if they had been asked to decide among specific cases of individuals who need money, rather than among funds or institutions?

How did the number of people who had to make the decision affect the decision-making process? Is it easier to decide working alone or is it more difficult, feeling the entire responsibility for the decision? Is an odd or even number of people in a group more effective for decision-making? What do you think would be the ideal way of distributing money collected for tzedakah?

List students' ideals for how to distribute on the blackboard under the heading "Ideal Ways of Distributing Money for Tzedakah."

Ask students how close they think this distributing experience has been to the reality of how people distribute money among charities today? What differences do they perceive?

3. Collection of tzedakah from students and discussion of elements of process.

Ask students how they think they would have responded to being asked to give money to a group of teenagers. What would they have wanted to know (about the collector, the cause, etc.) before they would have wanted to donate? Would the way they divided the money among the Tikun Olam tzedakot have been different if it was their own money?

Ask students to donate to Tikun Olam from out of their own pockets. Tell students that the funds that you collect will be given to Tikun Olam. (Note that every year, USY asks chapters to allocate where Tikun Olam money should be donated, but very few groups respond to this request.) Ask participants how they feel about someone they don't know deciding what to do with their money? Encourage them to select the tzedakah recipients rather than having the USY Tikun Olam Allocations Committee do it for them!

4.   Text study: Talmudic texts that describe the process of collecting and distributing money.

Begin by asking all students to fill out the "Needs of the Poor" on page 92. Select a number of texts from those printed on pages 93-104 that you think will interest your students and engage them in a discussion about traditional attitudes towards collecting and distributing tzedakah.

The texts on page 93 relate directly to the "Collection" and "Distribution" activities. They should be studied first by all students and compared to their own experiences with the activities described.

Follow this procedure for studying the texts on pages 93-104:
   a. Read the text silently or aloud.
   b. Have students paraphrase the text.
   c. What difficulties are there in the text that hinder students' understanding of it.
   d. To whom does the text show sensitivity? To whom does it show insensitivity?
   e. What does the text teach about giving tzedakah? What specific tzedakah-giving procedure does the text address?
   f. How do students feel about the message of the text? Is it still a valid message for the 20th century?

5.   Discussion: How do the talmudic texts relate to the biblical verse, "Love your neighbor as yourself"?

Ask students to review the texts they have studied and to relate each to the verse, "Love your neighbor as yourself." What is the nature of the love shown in the texts? How is the way the texts teach us to treat the poor like the way we might want to be treated if we were poor?

6. <u>Write guidelines for how to collect and distribute money for tzedakah.</u>

Divide the class into 4 groups. Give the following assignment:

Utilizing your experience from the collecting and distributing experiences and from discussing the texts from the Talmud, establish a list of guidelines which you consider to be the best ways to collect and distribute money for tzedakah. Work as a group to establish these guidelines. Write a rough draft on a piece of scrap paper. Then decide upon an order of priority for your guidelines; number 1 should be the guideline you think is most important; number 10, the one you think least important. When you have decided upon the guidelines and upon the priorities, copy them into your sourcebooks on page 105.

While students begin the work, write the specific directions for the assignment on the blackboard so that students can refer to them while they work.

Ask each group to record its final lists of guidelines and priorities on a piece of newsprint. Display the lists on the walls around the room. If there is time, ask each group to explain the decisions its members made in order to arrive at their final lists. If time is limited, explain that the newsprint lists will be posted and that students will have an opportunity to exchange ideas and discuss them during the next session.

UNIT 2

Objectives:

a. Students will be able to list examples of the way those who wrote a number of medieval codes of Jewish law encouraged sensitivity to the needs of the poor.

b. Students will be able to compare and contrast guidelines for giving and collecting tzedakah that they wrote during Unit 1 with the guidelines written by the authors of the medieval codes.

Outline of the Unit:

1. Text Study: "Ladders of Tzedakah" written by Maimonides, Moses b. Jacob of Coucy, Al-Nakawa.

2. Compare and contrast the medieval texts with the guidelines written by students during Unit 1.

3. Compare and contrast the ladders of tzedakah of each of the medievalists.

4. Compare and contrast the medieval texts with the talmudic texts.

Remember to post the newsprint lists of student guidelines for how to collect and distribute tzedakah!

1. <u>Text study</u>: "<u>Ladders of Tzedakah</u>" <u>written</u> <u>by</u> <u>Maimonides</u>, <u>Moses</u> <u>ben</u> <u>Jacob</u> <u>of</u> <u>Coucy</u>, <u>and</u> <u>Al-Nakawa</u>.

   Divide students into the same four groups in which they worked during the last lesson. Assign each of the groups one of the medieval "ladders of tzedakah" on pages 106-109. Each group should do the following work with its "ladder of tzedakah":

   a. Read all the steps on the ladder and copy them onto newsprint.
   b. Develop a dramatization of each of the steps on the ladder.
   c. Discuss why each step is higher or lower than the next.
   d. Discuss how the ladder show sensitivity to the <u>needs</u> of the recipient; to the <u>feelings</u> of the donor and to the <u>feelings</u> of the recipient.

2. <u>Compare</u> <u>and</u> <u>contrast</u> <u>the</u> <u>ladder</u> <u>with</u> <u>the</u> <u>guidelines</u> <u>written</u> <u>by</u> <u>the</u> <u>group</u> <u>during</u> <u>the</u> <u>previous</u> <u>lesson</u>.

   Post the newsprint "ladders" next to the students' guidelines. When the groups have completed these tasks, ask them to present the results of their work on the steps above. After one group completes one of the steps allow other students to react to what has been presented, to ask questions, offer alternative explanations, etc.

3. <u>Compare</u> <u>and</u> <u>contrast</u> <u>the</u> <u>ladders</u> <u>of</u> <u>tzedakah</u> <u>of</u> <u>each</u> <u>of</u> <u>the</u> <u>medievalists</u>.

   Ask the students to list the common elements found in the ladders and to list those elements which are unique to any of the ladders. List these elements on the blackboard. Include structural elements (i.e., descending or ascending order). Ask students why they think Moses b. Jacob and Al-Nakawa found it necessary to write their own "ladders" even though Maimonides had written his ladder many years earlier, and why Al-Nakawa felt it necessary to write two ladders. How do the 3 other ladders compare with the work Maimonides did? Is there a ladder that the students prefer? Is there a ladder or a point on a ladder that seems to fit contemporary needs better than the others? Are there points on the ladders that no longer need to be taken into consideration in modern times? Are some categories omitted (such as "not giving")?

4. <u>Compare</u> <u>and</u> <u>contrast</u> <u>the</u> <u>medieval</u> <u>texts</u> <u>and</u> <u>the</u> <u>talmudic</u> <u>texts</u>.

   Ask the students to review the talmudic materials on pages 93-104 to see if they can find any texts that seem related to the medieval materials. What talmudic ideas are reflected in the medieval ladders? Are there talmudic ideas that seem to have been disregarded by the medievalists (either contradicted or ignored)? Are there any creative or innovative ideas in the medieval ladders that are not considered in any of the talmudic texts in our sourcebook? (The sourcebook is not exhaustive of the texts from the talmudic period that might be precursors to the medieval ladders.)

   <u>At</u> <u>the</u> <u>end</u> <u>of</u> <u>the</u> <u>lesson</u>: Allow the students to meet in their small groups to revise their guidelines for tzedakah in light of Unit 2.

UNIT 3

Objectives:

a. Students will be to evalute contemporary methods
   of collecting money and distributing it to the
   poor by the standards of traditional Jewish
   guidelines from the Talmud and the codes.

b. Students will decide on their own future involvement
   with tzedakah and will plan future meetings and
   activities concerning tzedakah.

Outline of Unit:

1. Compare and contrast the work of UJA and Federations
   with the traditional means by which Jews supported
   the poor.

2. Compare and contrast the work of Tzedakah Collectives
   with the traditional means by which Jews supported
   the poor.

3. Compare and contrast the Tikun Olam program with the
   traditional approaches.

4. Discuss other means of supporting the poor about which
   students have information.

5. Discussion: The needs of the poor--who can satisfy
   them?

6. Class decision-making: What is the response of
   the class to the needs of the poor?

Unit 3

1. Compare and contrast the work of UJA and Federations with the traditional means by which Jews supported the poor.

   The listing on pages 110-112 shows the scope of Federation-supported projects.

2. Compare and contrast the work of Tzedakah Collectives with the traditional means by which Jews supported the poor.

3. Consider the Tikun Olam program and how it compares with the traditional approaches.

   Divide the class into three new groups. Assign one group to study the work of the UJA and Federations, one group to study the work of Tzedakah Collectives (pp. 113-114) and one to study Tikun Olam. After reading and discussing the material in the sourcebook about these topics, students may decide that they would like to learn more about these means of supporting the needy in the Jewish community. They should be encouraged to do further research into the topics and to invite guest speakers to address the entire class about UJA and Federations, Tzedakah Collectives, Tikun Olam and other philanthropic Jewish organizations in existence today.

   After the various philantropies have been discussed, speakers heard, research done, etc., ask students to compare and contrast the modern philanthropic agencies with the traditional Jewish means of supporting the poor. Which of the modern methods studied most closely approximates the traditional ways of helping the poor? How do modern methods show sensitivity towards the needs of the donor, the recepient and the collector? Do they show insensitivity?

4. Discuss other means of supporting the poor about which students have information.

5. Discussion: The needs of the poor--who can satisfy them?

Ask the students to review and add to the form on page 92. Ask them to share their ideas. Of these needs that individuals could satisfy, with which do the students think that they might be able to help? Of those that the community agencies could satisfy, do students see that they might be able to play a part in those agencies? Are any new agencies needed?

NOTE: Tzedakah boxes in the home and synagogue have provided a means for giving tzedakah to masses of Jewish people. You might suggest to the participants that donating in this manner (putting money in the "pushka") can be a daily way to recognize the needs of the poor and help fulfill our responsibility.

6. Class decision-making: What is the response of the class to the needs of the poor?

Students have noted areas of need which they believe they could help in satisfying. Discuss what the class should do about tzedakah. Is it sufficient to have studied the topic? Should students (and teacher) become involved in helping to solve some of the problems of the poor? How?

Some suggestions:

a. Encourage the class to become a Tzedakah Collective or to function as part of the Tikun Olam Program. Plan a calendar of meetings; establish committees to research various causes and funds; invite guest speakers and contribute money--either students' own money or funds raised by group for tzedakah.

b. Try to visit the local Federation and its agencies. Find out how the group can become involved in at least one type of tzedakah program.

THE GREATEST KINDNESS--ḤESED SHEL EMET--חֶסֶד שֶׁל אֱמֶת

INTRODUCTION

UNIT 1

Objectives: a. Students should be able to list Jewish
               practices that give honor to the dead;

            b. Students should be able to define the
               work of the Ḥevrah Kaddisha.

There are a number of ways to achieve the objectives of this
lesson which are not included in the recommended lesson plan. A
combination of the recommended lesson plan with additional strategies (suggested below) would be the idea approach to achieve the
objective.

Additional strategies:

   The congregational rabbi, a member of the local Hevrah Kaddisha,
   or an ethical funeral director could visit the class to discuss
   these issues and to be interviewed by the class.

   Students might visit the funeral home and the cemetery (to bury
   books) in order to sense some of the values being taught in
   this unit.

   Ultimately (in Unit 3) students will discuss the need for and
   work of the Ḥevrah Kaddisha in greater depth--and consider
   their own potential participation.

Outline of Unit 1:

1. Focus on the problem: exercise to deal with decisions and
    emotions at the time of the death of a loves one.

2. Discussion of students' personal experiences with death
    and mourning.

3. Text study: Giving honor to the dead.

4. Text study: The work of the Ḥevrah Kaddisha.

5. Analysis:What abuses might occur if there is no Ḥevrah Kaddisha?

6. Summary: How does the Jewish community give honor to the dead?

NOTE: Students who have suffered the deaths of close relatives
should be approached individually and given the option of not
attending these class sessions. If such students do want to attend
these sessions, they should be consulted about how they would like
to participate so that they are comfortable and not needlessly
distressed. (Also see the *NOTES* on T-26, T-27 for additional guide-
and in this regard.)

1. <u>Focus on the problem</u>.

   The climate in the clasroom during the sessions dealing with death (as well as all other sessions!) must be one in which students feel safe to reveal fears and emotions about facing death--both their own and the death of loved ones. Students must feel that they will not be criticized or ridiculed for expressing themselves openly.

   Ask students to turn to page 120. Tell them to work in pairs discussing the exercise "When a person dies, his close relatives are faced with two tasks," and then filling in the chart of "Decisions" and "Emotions." When students have completed this work, ask each student to explain one of the issues he has noted, beginning with "Decisions" and then going on to "Emotions." This discussion should flow directly into the next section of the unit-- the discussion of students' personal experiences with death and mourning.

   It is assumed that students will want to exchange experiences and ideas that they have about death and mourning. This exchange is to be welcomed, inasmuch as it will help students to recognize the importance and relevance of the topic to their own lives. Their recollections are likely to be random and related in numerous ways to the topic. Allow the exchange to continue for a few minutes, and then try to focus on issues discussed that relate specifically to the topic of this unit, that is, how the <u>community</u> helps (or in their experience, hinders) the dead and the <u>mourners</u>. (The subject of this unit is not, for example, "mourning" or "what happens when you die." Students may discuss issues like these because they are important to them. Eventually, however, the discussion must be focused on the topic of <u>community</u> involvement.

2. <u>Discussion of students' personal experience with death and mourning</u>. If the exercise on page 120 has not elicited from students discussion about their own experience, ask students if they have ever attended a funeral or visited a house where people were sitting Shivah. What happened at the funeral or at the Shivah house?
   Summarize by noting that by attending a funeral, students have practiced an important act of gemilut ḥasadim.

3. <u>Text study: Giving honor to the dead</u>.

   a. Read the text from Genesis 47:29. Provide the historical background if students are unsure of the context. Note Rashi's comment to the biblical text.

   Why is burying the dead the highest form of lovingkindness-- ḥesed shel emet?

   b. Read and analyze the text from Mo'ed Katan. Ask students to differentiate between the actions discussed in the text that give dignity to the living and those that show honor for the dead.

   Does this text really show that the Rabbis wanted to honor the dead? Ask students for pros and cons.
   Why did the decisions of the Rabbis in this text always favor the sensitivities of the poor? What do you think they were trying to say about the nature of death-- and to <u>some</u> extent-- about the nature of life?

   (All men are equal in death; they should be treated equally not only in death but also in life.)

c. Do an exercise of comparison with students as an introduction
to the material on pages 121-122.

How is a person like a Sefer Torah?
(See the note on T-10 about a synectic exercise.)

Let participants brainstorm possible similarities. Then ask
them to read the top paragraph on page 121. What does this
paragraph describe as the similarity of a person and a Sefer
Torah? How do you feel about this comparison?

Assign an equal number of students to read each of the nine
sections of the text (pages 121-122) Each student should read
his selection carefully and be prepared to explain its contents
to the rest of the class.

Ask one of the students who read paragraph #1 to explain it to the
class. Answer questions and clarify areas where students are
unsure of the meaning. Continue with #2 and so forth.

Review each of the points and ask, "How does this action or
behavior show honor for the deceased?" Be prepared for some
students to object and to say that they think certain items
do not show honor. Ask them to explain their thinking.

Tell students that as they study the traditional Jewish ideas
toward these issues, they will have a chance to review their
positions and to consider them again.

d. Ask a student to read the section of the Funeral Service (page 122) alound. Again, ask students to refer to the criteria of giving honor to the dead, and ask them how the Jewish funeral measures on the criteria.

e. Ask a student to read the section of The Burial (page 122) aloud. How does the burial conform to the notion of giving honor to the dead? Does it fit in better with the notion of comforting the mourners? Is it a special category of its own?

(Perhaps it is in a special category: while the burial is required for the dignity of the dead, and while seeing their loved one safely laid to rest may comfort the mourner, the burial probably serves as the "rudest awakener"--the activity surrounding death that emphasizes in most stunning fashion that the person has truly died and will not return.)

f. Draw a chart on the blackboard. Put "Honors the Dead" on one side and "Comforts Mourners" on the other. Ask students to fill in as many points as they can on either side of the chart.

4. <u>Text study: The work of the Ḥevrah Kaddisha.</u>

a. Ask students who does all the work that needs to
be done in order to properly bury the dead?

Note that at one time, everyone in town was affected
when someone died; to some extent, they all helped
bury the dead.

Read the text on page 123 from Mo'ed Katan 27b.

What did Rav Hamnuna want to do to the people of Daru-matha?

What law did he think they were transgressing?

What did the people of the town of Daru-matha know that
Rav Hamnuna did not know?

When they shared this knowledge with him, was he satisfied
that they were not guilty of wrongdoing?

What do you think that the Ḥevrah Kaddisha did--in Daru-
matha or elsewhere--that exempted the rest of the town
from their traditional responsibilities?

b. Read the Dresner excerpt on pages 123-124. Ask
students to infer from this article how a Ḥevrah Kaddisha
would function in modern times--and what differences, if
any, they would think there might have been in the work
of the Ḥevrah Kaddisha in the in the past.

c. Read the Dresner excerpt on the bottom of page 124.
What is the relationship of the community to the Ḥevrah
Kaddisha?

Do you think it was an honor to be a member of the Ḥevrah
Kaddisha? How would you feel about being a member of
a Ḥevrah Kaddisha?

5.   Analysis: What abuses might occur if there is no
Ḥevrah Kaddisha?

Ask students to reconsider the concepts and laws from the
reading on pages 121-122 and to review the requirements for
proper care of the body and its burial according to Jewish
law. What kinds of abuses might occur if there is no Ḥevrah
Kaddisha? Why do you think they might occur? How might
a Ḥevrah Kaddisha prevent them?

6.   Summary: How does the Jewish community give honor
to the dead?

Add any additional items to the chart on the board that
students may have thought of during the last part of the
lesson. Review by asking students to summarize the points
in the chart.

(Retain the chart for use during the next lesson.)

Unit 2

Objectives: a. students will be able to list the relatives of the deceased that are mourners according to Jewish law;
b. students should be able to list Jewish mourning practices that show sensitivity to the mourners.

Outline of Unit 2:

1. Definition: who are the relatives for whom Jews are required to mourn?
2. Text Study: the treatment of mourners.
3. Movie: *A Plain Pine Box.*
4. Discussion and reaction to the movie.

1. Definition: who are the relatives for whom Jews are required to mourn?

List on the blackboard a number of relatives, including those for whom Jews are required to mourn. For example:

father	half-sister	aunt
mother	half-brother	uncle
grandfather	husband	nephew
grandmother	wife	neice
sister	grandchild	mother-in-law
brother	son	father-in-law
cousin	daughter	

Ask students to note (in the margin of the student booklet) for which of these relatives Jews are required to mourn.

Do a quick survey (thumbs up or hands raised) of how many students believe each of the relatives listed above is one for whom Jews are required to mourn. Note the number of students who think each of the above is one of the required relatives. Ask students to defend their beliefs: why do they think these are the relatives for whom Jews mourn?

Explain that there are only seven relatives for whom we are required to mourn.* That does not mean that we ignore or are insensitive to the deaths of other relatives, or that if students know of people who have (or have themselves) mourned for others than these seven that they have done anything wrong. Nevertheless, the specific rules of Keriah, Shivah, and Shloshim, and the recitation of Kaddish, apply only to these seven.

Erase the relatives who are not among the seven in the list above.

* Those relatives for whom we are required to mourn are: Parents (mother, father); spouse (husband/wife); sibling (brother, sister); child (son, daughter). We use the number 7 rather than 8 since any given mourner cannot have both a husband and wife.

Ask students to read the text on page 125 from Leviticus.

How is this text related to the issue of relatives for whom we mourn?
(These are the relatives for whom the Kohanim were allowed to come in contact with any other dead body. The rabbis adopted this definition for determining which relationships were the closest and for whom we mourn.)

What characteristics are common to these relationships?
(Parents and children are direct blood relatives; siblings are indirect blood relationships; spouses are life partners--not common to other relationships.)

Are there other relatives that you think should be included?

Do you understand why they were not traditionally included?

Ask students to fill in the box on page 125: "For which relatives do we mourn?"

2. Recite the first text on page 125 ("When you hear of a death...") Recite the words "Baruch dayyan ha-emet" together as a class. Recite the words "Blessed be the Righteous Judge."

Ask students how they would feel saying these words upon hearing about the death of someone they knew? of a close relative?

Ask for personal interpretations of what these words mean.

Explain that one way of understanding these words is that they acknowledge the fact that there are some things in life that we as human beings have no control over. Death is surely one of those things. For those who might feel guilt or reponsibility upon hearing of the death of someone they knew, saying these words is a recognition that they personally had nothing to do with causing the death. For those who are less intimately involved, the words are a reminder that people do not control the time of death -- and are not in control of many things that are central to the human experience.

3. Read the text from Pirke Avot on page 125

What does "and confort him not when his dead lies before him" mean? Aren't we supposed to comfort mourners?

(The focus is on the words "lies before him   This means that we should not try to comfort mourners prior to the funeral and burial of the dead.)

Why shouldn't we try to comfort mourners prior to the funeral and burial?

(This is the time of the most intense grief for which there is no comfort: there are important arrangements to be made; the family needs to be alone to try to handle their private emotional responses to the death.)

Write the terms אֲנִינוּת and אוֹנֵן on the blackboard. Ask students to define them if they have heard of them; otherwise explain these terms using the following article to form your definitions:

The period of mourning is divided into two phases:
  a. The time between the moment of death and the interment of the body.
  b. The time after the interment of the body to the end of Shivah, and the less intense subsequent forms of mourning.
The first phase is called Aninut and the second, Avelut.

ANINUT
During the period of Aninut the mourner (not yet technically a mourner, called an Onen) is legally exempt from the performance of all religious obligations such as recitation of the morning and evening prayers or putting on tefillin. At the same time, one is forbidden to drink wine, eat meat, or indulge in luxuries.

The reason for these prescriptions is twofold. First, there is the general principle, "He who is occupied with the performance of a Mitzvah is exempt from the performance of another Mitzvah." Since the mourner must attend to the needs of the deceased, there should be nothing to distract him from this obligation, and it takes precedence. Second, it is considered a breach of K'vod Hamet to do anything but attend to the deceased. Hence, even if the mourner wants to perform his religious obligations (though exempt), he is not permitted to do so.
                    Isaac Klein, *A Time to Be Born, a Time to Die* (New York: United Synagogue Youth, 1976), pp. 31-32.

Read the text from Mo'ed Katan 28b on page 125. What does this text teach us about behavior in a house of mourning?

Have you ever felt obligated to speak when visiting a mourner? Why?

Does the atmosphere in most places where you have visited mourners reflect this teaching? If not, why do you think a different atmosphere prevails?

3. (cont.)

Ask students to read the remaining paragraphs on pages 126-127 silently. When they have finished, ask them to add to the chart on the board (from the previous lesson) under the heading "comforting mourners." What are the aspects of Jewish law that deal with comforting mourners? How to they act to give comfort?

Ask students to recite the sentence

   "Ha-Makom Yenaḥem..."

Ask them to recite the sentence in English.

How does this sentence give comfort to mourners? How do you feel when you say it? How would you feel to hear someone say it to you?

Why do you think Jewish tradition insists on specific mourning practices and behaviors in comforting mourners? Wouldn't it be best simply to allow every mourner and comforting visitor to do what they want to do naturally?

Allow this discussion to be open-ended. If none of the students points out the strong, positive points in favor of requirements for mourning and for how to give comfort, note some of them and let students react to them. For example, mourners should not have to think about what to do when they are in such distress. Visitors sometimes are insensitive when they want very much to be sensitive. The rules set down in the tradition help a visitor to show sensitivity to the mourner.

4. Movie: *A Plain Pine Box*. (Available from *The Eternal Light*, 155 Fifth Avenue, New York, N.Y. 10010.)

5. Discussion and reaction to the movie.

Be sure to deal with these issues:

a. What moved the people in this congregation for form their own Ḥevrah Kaddisha?
b. What does the Ḥevrah Kaddisha do for the deceased?
c. What does the Ḥevrah Kaddisha do for the mourners?
d. During what time period is the Ḥevrah Kaddisha involved with the mourners?
e. Why did a congregation consider it their responsibility to become a Ḥevrah Kaddisha? Do you believe such a function should be in the domain of a synagogue or congregation?

UNIT 3

Objectives:

    a. Students should be able to evaluate modern
       alternatives for attending the dead from the
       moment of death until burial and for comforting
       the mourners against the standard of the tradi-
       tional requirements of Jewish law;

    b. Students should be able to decide on what
       functions of a Ḥevrah Kaddisha their class
       could carry out--and do them.

Outline of Unit:

    1. Review main points of the movie, *A Plain Pine Box*.

    2. Text study: Standards for funerals at Congregation
       Beth El.

    3. Text study: Description of funeral home services.

    4. Simulation: The membership of a congregation must
       decide on how to deal with funeral practices in
       its community.

    5. Discussion: Should or could the class form a
       Ḥevrah Kaddisha--and what aspects of Ḥevrah
       Kaddisha work could it do. Establish a plan.

1. Review main points of the movie, *A Plain Pine Box*.

    Note some of the issues that came out in the
discussion following the movie, and the basic decision that the people in Minneapolis made concerning
funeral practices in their city. This review should
take no more than five minutes.

2. **Text study: Standards for funerals in one community.**

Read the article on page 130 about the Beth El alternative.

What are the rabbi and congregation proposing? Who must follow the regulations regarding funeral and mourning practices?

How do you think these regulations can be enforced?

How would you feel if you belonged to Beth El and knew that you, as a Jew, would have to abide by these rules in case of a death in your family?

3. <u>Text study: Description of funeral home services.</u>

Read the advertisement on page 131.

What is this funeral home saying about how the dead should
be treated and buried?
   (Each individual family makes its own decisions, based
    on financial and other considerations.)

Are there any regulations about Jewish practices that must
be followed at the funeral home?

Is there anything distinctly Jewish about this funeral home?

How would you feel if you lived in a city where this funeral
home was the only "Jewish" funeral home.

   NOTE: This is not a polemic against **all** Jewish funeral
          homes!

4. <u>Simulation: Funeral practices in our community.</u>

Assign in advance a few students to key roles in the congregation meeting that will be simulated--for example, the rabbi,
the ritual chairman, someone who will introduce the Beth El
alternative, someone who will introduce the Minneapolis alternative, and the local funeral director (who is a member of
the congregation).

The topic of discussion at the meeting is
      What can this congregation do to insure that the
      spirit of the Jewish laws about honoring the dead
      and comforting the mourners is upheld in this community?

Tell students that they may choose to support any of the
options discussed at the meeting--or may introduce new options
that have not been considered. Encourage them to refer to
sources in the sourcebook to support their positions.

Participate in the meeting yourself as a concerned congregant.

Arrange in advance with whoever is playing the role of the
rabbi to limit the simulation to a maximum of 30 minutes
(20 may be sufficient).

Discuss with the participants the possibility of their
inquiring about the funeral practices in Jewish funeral homes
in their community. How would they go about getting this
information?

5. Discussion: <u>What should this class do?</u>

This discussion would serve to debrief the simulation to some extent. Ask students to relate to the ideas discussed on a personal level: What should the funeral and mourning practices in their city be?

What should they do in order to influence these practices?

Review the chart on the blackboard (from previous lessons). What could teenagers do that would give honor to the dead and comfort the mourners?

Decide on a plan of action for the group. It might even be an investigation of the local Jewish funeral homes or--even though there might be no abuses--it might be a commitment to treat every death of a friend, acquaintance, or congregant in a personal way--like helping to form shivah minyanim, visiting mourners, etc.

Record decisions on page 133. Refer to them as the plan of action is implemented.

SUMMARY CHAPTER

Objectives:

a. Participants will be able to list the community service activities in which they have participated;

b. Participants will be able to discuss how their participation in community service activities has influenced their feelings about the values of tzedakah and gemilut ḥasadim;

c. Participants will be able to write a paragraph, similar to an "ethical will," which describes the values they consider to be the most important in life that they would like to pass on or teach to other people.

Outline of Chapter

1. List community service activities in which the students have participated.

2. Review the concepts of tzedakah and gemilut ḥasadim.

3. Discussion: How has participating in community service activities influenced students' feelings about doing acts of tzedakah and gemilut ḥasadim?

4. Text study: Medieval and modern ethical wills.

5. Introspection about personal values.

1. <u>List community service activities in which the students
have participated.</u>

Ask students to work in pairs and to list all the community
service activities in which they or the group have participated during the course of studying *Tzorchei Tzibbur*. Use
the framework provided on page 135 for organizing students'
recollections of their activities.

2. <u>Review the concepts of tzedakah and gemilut hasadim.</u>

Ask students to review the early pages of the sourcebook
(pages 4-7) that deal with defining these concepts. Now
that they have had some personal experience with a number
of mitzvot that fall into these categories, what do they
feel are the real differences between these two ideas?
Is it easier to perform acts of tzedakah or gemilut
hasadim? What is difficult about doing these acts?

What do we learn about the Jewish people by knowing that
they value highly both tzedakah and gemilut hasadim? Are
these values that every generation of Jews should be
taught about?

3. Discussion: <u>How has participating in community service
activities influenced students' feelings about doing
acts of tzedakah and gemilut hasadim?</u>

Ask students what they have learned by participating in
the service activities that they might not have learned
if they had only read the sourcebook without the opportunity to perform some of these mitzvot. How did they
feel as they participated in the various service activities? Why do they think the Jewish people has considered these mitzvot to be important elements of community
life? Would students consider doing these mitzvot again,
outside of the class framework? Why? Why not?

4. <u>Text study: Medieval and modern ethical wills.</u>

Ask students to read the selection on page 136 by Albert
Vorspan. Discuss what Vorspan is suggesting:

What do you ordinarily expect someone to write in a will?
Why are these things that people write in wills? What
different kind of will did our ancestors write?

It is interesting to note that some people did not only
write wills to help in guiding their children after their
deaths, but also wrote testaments to guide their own lives!

Ask students to read each of the selections from the ethical wills on pages 137-141. What are the values that the authors consider to be most important? Ask students if they agree or disagree with these values. Should these values still be cherished in the 20th century?

After discussing each selection, ask the students to note their own feelings in the space provided below each selection, comparing them with the values each author considered important.

Ask students to indicate in their notes the values they believe their own parents would endorse. Ask them to think (silently and privately) about how they would feel if their parents wrote a will containing similar ideas.

The last selection ("A Regimen of Self-Taxation," pages 140-141) shows how one man took the value of tzedakah seriously in his own life. How does this commitment differ from the writing of an ethical will that "binds" one's children to the values he held in life?

Inasmuch as students are more involved in shaping their own lives and value systems than trying to "bind" future generations, the exercises students will be asked to complete at the end of this chapter deal with personal introspection in developing a guide of ethical principles for themselves.

5. Introspection about personal values.

Tell students that this exercise is private and need not be shared with anyone. Ask students to consider what values in life they think are most important. Remind them of the mitzvot they have studied in *Tzorchei Tzibbur* and of value issues they have discussed during the course of study.

Ask students to write their own proposals for the values that should guide their lives. They could phrase their suggestions in the terminology of a will (instructions for children who will remain after the author dies) or they could describe a program for their own behavior as Jewish adults.

Ask students to keep the *Tzorchei Tzibbur* sourcebook and to review the work they did in it from time to time. They might want to take the advice of Solomon ben Isaac, and read their "testaments" regularly--once a month or once a week. Encourage them to add to their "proposals for ethical living" even after they have left the class, youth group, and high school environment. If they do so and actively come to understand who they are, they will learn a great deal about who they once were!

If participants want to discuss their "Personal Values" work, use these questions to guide the discussion:

> Can you analyze the process by which you arrived at your decisions?
> Are you happy with the process? Are you happy with the results (=your decisions)?
> To what extent were the sources valuable, not valuable, or irrelevant (helpful/confusing/irrelevant)? Why?
> To what extent were the activities helpful/confusing/irrelevant?
> To what extent were the discussions helpful/confusing/irrelevant? Why?

FINAL NOTE TO THE TEACHER: Hopefully you have participated in all aspects of the program that you required of your students--and you have written your own ethical will.

Have you changed your values as a result of interaction with students?

Have you learned anything new about yourself, your students, or Judaism as a result of participating in this program? Have you had good feelings about some sources, activities, discussions? Bad feelings? No feelings?

In analyzing the success or failure of this program, consider both your students' responses to these questions, and your own.